Donald —

Thank you for the books you have sent to me. Here's one in return.

I'm looking forward to the Tom/Kim/Carol and your volume born out of your poetry workshop long ago.

Best to you —

Paul

2023

In the River of My Sleep

Paul Dresman

In the River of My Sleep by Paul Dresman.
First Edition.
March 2023.
All rights reserved.

Front cover:
Ron Wigginton (1944 -

Libra, 2020.
Co-polymer, sumi ink, pencil, metallics.
Vintage Japanese paper 29" x 22" irregular.
Layout and cover design: Silvana Pezoa N.

Library of Congress Control Number: 9781736178492

ISBN: 978-1-7361784-9-2

Editorial El Sur es América, LLC.
Athens, Ohio, USA.
ElSurEsAmerica@gmail.com
www.EditorialElSurEsAmerica.com

In the River of My Sleep

New and Selected Poems

and occasional prose

by

Paul Dresman

Acknowledgments

- The third section of "Diving Deep" was originally published as "Maybe I Should Throw Them a Poem", *Into the Teeth of the Wind*, University of Calif. at Santa Barbara, 2004.
- "Diving Deep" (under the title, "A River Running to the Sea") won the poetry award of the 2020 San Miguel de Allende Writers Conference and was published on the conference website in Mexico. It also appeared in the bilingual anthology *Fuego Cruzado*.
- "Transcontinental Drift" was published under the title "Slatches" in *Catamaran*, Santa Cruz, California, June, 2020.
- "Cleaning Woman" was published in *Poetry International*, San Diego State University, 1999.
- The first section of "California Frontage" was published in *Green Anarchy*, Eugene, 1995 under the title "Hegelian Cartography" and in *Peter's Pen Pals*, Rancho Santa Fe, 1983.
- "Killing Floor" appeared in *Americas Review*, Berkeley and Davis, California, 2000.
- The first part of "Ode to Internal Combustion" came out as "Drags" in *Antenna*, San Diego, 1978 and the third part in *Ocean Hiway*, an anthology, Wild Mustard Press, La Mesa, 1985.
- "War Poems" was published in *Reed Magazine*, San Jose State University, 2021.
- A part of "Coda" originally appeared in *Crazy Quilt* titled "Underground and Indigo-Blue," San Diego, California, 1987.
- In "Dangerous Ideas," the sixth movement, "Crow Woman's Song,"'appeared in *San Diego* magazine, February, 1983. The seventh— "If Jack Wilson...."— came out in *Cincinnati Poetry Review*, 1984, under the tile "Parallel and Telling." Part of the final section "Across from the burned-out reservation motel..." appeared in *South Dakota Review*, University of South Dakota, 1985, as the poem "Willow Work.".
- "A Silver Gelatin Photograph of Grand Central Station, 1934" in *Terra Incognita*, New York, 1999.
- "Poets in the Streets" appeared on the *Blog* at Flying Ketchup Press website, Kansas City, 2021. The poem included in this account, "You Kissed Us Both," appeared in Rolling Stone, San Francisco, February, 1971.
- The second part of "Lost Chalkline" appeared as a poem in *Hawaii Pacific Review*, Honolulu, Hawaii, 1988.

- Several parts of "Archipelago" were published as a lyrical essay in *The Eastern Iowa Review*, 2019.
- "Momentary Poems from China" appeared in *Square One*, University of Colorado at Boulder, 1999 and in different form in *The Eugene Weekly*, 1990.
- "The Uses of Poetry" appeared in the anthology, *Small Rain*, Eight Poets from San Diego, D.G. Wills Books, La Jolla, 1985.
- "School Business" was first published in *Mud Creek*, Portland, Oregon, 1989.
- "Lookout!," "Extinctions," and "Where Do We Go From Here?" First appeared in the anthology *The End of the World Project* under the title: Five Poems for the End of Time, 2018.
- Along with "Cante Jondo" and "Running to the Sea," the above three poems also appeared in English and Spanish in the bilingual anthology *Fuego Cruzado/Crossfire*, edited by Amado Lascar, (several translators), El Sur es America Press, Ohio, September, 2020.
- "Cante Jondo" first came out as a five-page lyrical essay on the *Permafrost* website, University of Alaska at Fairbanks, 2018. Now it is a short poem.
- "Night Work" was first published in *Bad Light*, Portland, Oregon, 2008.
- "John Reed's Lost Poem" was first published in *helicóptero*, Eugene, 1994.
- "Inferno in the American Forest" was published in. the anthology The Great Pause: Rearview 2020, Post Pause Press, Wilmington, North Carolina, 2022.
- "Under the Dome" was published in the anthology, *The Very Edge*, of artists and poets in Spanish, French, and English, by Flying Ketchup Press, Kansas City, August, 2020.

Guide

Babylonian Radio

In the Water

Prologue

The weather deepens roots, and I write from an American imagination, a subterranean spirit in cahoots with wellsprings and camaraderie.

There is a river in my sleep, a river in my life. This book follows the course from a wonderous but instructive childhood in the near desert of southern California to my eightieth year a thousand miles north in a fertile valley of many rivers.

In poetry and occasional prose I revisit experiences in Europe, China, Latin America where the rapid currents and the slow depths of people and culture enhanced and defined my life and outlook.

In fact, a group of Chileans who come from that nation of poetry giants at the antipodes brought this book into being. Thank you, Jesús, thank you, Amado, thank you, Silvana.

A river might flow temporally and eternally through finite time and infinite space. History is a nightmare I am trying to elucidate, poetry the singing, invisible flag I raise.

Paul Dresman
Oregon
2023

In the River of My Sleep

For Christine, my wife, lover, and best friend,
mother of our children, fifty years
together, let's dance.

Diving Deep

I am inside a boat turned-over,
one of a trillion drops of cloud.
Everyone knows water can't speak.
That's why I write on water-
to put words in its mouth.
Now it says we're bound for the depths,
and there I am, cavorting at the bow.

*

Before I was sweat, I was blood.
Before I was urine, I was pure.
Before I was man, I was woman.
Before I was warmed by the sun,

I was pulled this way
and that way by the moon.

*

The sea appears in dream after dream.
The shore's forever relative.
Waves rush inland over streets.
Buildings go under. The car submerges
just out of reach, and my family's faces
look out the rear window. They're hoping
I can stop it before they're taken away.
They beg to be saved.

But I can't help- I'm asleep.
*

A rotund kid, thirteen years-old, jumps off the high dive and drops like a stone. I think he's joking- a little game played for his friends. He remains, and I look off to tell someone to stop running, take time to glance into the corner shadows in case someone small has slipped and disappeared.

When I look back, the kid's still there.
You don't even think about what you're doing. You're off the tower, gone through the air in a dive, slicing the water, the momentum

17

carrying you down to where he lies still on the bottom by the main drain. I grab him: limp, dead weight. When I push off the concrete, we go up a little too slowly. He must weigh as much as I do. I kick and kick but he's a handful, so I stop the struggle, relax, let us go down.

This time I coil to spring hard, shoot up easily the whole twelve feet. Without thinking, I have him in the proper grip, my right arm hooked under his arm, across his chest, my left hand for swimming or, if he tries to resist, to hold him steady, while I kick across the pool. Reaching the gutter, grabbing it, I catch a whiff of his breath: Model airplane glue.

Drooling puke, he says, *"No vale la pena."*
Two other lifeguards pull him up onto the deck,
carry him to the pool office.
In the wake of it, shocked by the rush, shaking, back in the world, East L.A., 1962, an ambulance arriving, a siren, a life to be lost if it could be saved.
Glue wing struts to the fuselage, doors to the bomb bay.

*

The young girls try so hard to be good.
The young men survive in gangs
that threaten their lives.
Maybe the poet could toss them a line,
maybe throw them a ring,
something round and sweet,
rich and strange
that suffers no sea-change.

Maybe try a scream,
down deep
where no one's listening.

Tumbleweeds

"I've got another of those damn thistles in my thumb," my Scot grandmother used to say, as she worked and squeezed with other fingers at a splinter lodged there. Her hands were red potatoes, her maiden name McBain. Every fall in L.A., or wherever I am, I remember everything loose tumbling past in the Santa Ana wind, and my grandmother's ancient hands— eroded alluvial fans.

Crowded into the working class condition, it was turning winter and the subtropical walls appeared to grow thin. The wind wound-up and whined the complaints of the age— the creaks, the hacks, the coughs that accompanied the wheezing pipes, squeezed border ballads of saber-to-belly thanes and harps made of sister's breastbone.

Cold nights, the portable gas heater brought close, we stared into the element as if it were a flickering peat fire on a stone hearth as seen through an insubstantial 20th century grill. My grandmother leaned over the sheep dog's belly in a house on a south central street in Los Angeles lined with palms. The dog was a black and white succeeder to a lineage always called Tinker, and she searched with her fingers to rid him of fleas. Poor fleas! Happy Tinker! You could draw a little human face later, at the far end of fate, for innocent predators caught, squeezed, popped by her fingers.

In another time— we were in another time, in highland meadow night with the old Bobby- poet of lang syne, while the velvety-white underbelly fur turned in swirls over the soft, pink, dog flesh beneath. The grateful dog's tongue lolled on red gums of white incisors. Wisps of my grandmother's thick broth of Scottish white hair fell forward and uplifted in the rising waves radiating from the heater. Accompanying her deep concentration, a distant glow of old, stand-alone radio, and Grandfather Jack in the aura of soft lamp and easy chair.

There were directions, indirections, a family that started and stopped, and started again in that loose world where we met, where we have always been cast adrift, thistles we brought with us, thistles that met us.

Transcontinental Drift

Sails and trails on the whale's path,
depths caught in tone-talk.
I can hear incisions
carved in scrimshaw.

In a moment and forever, too,
ghosts and their echoes
feedback into loops—
winds, runes.

*

From a perspective below the long work bench-golden curls
of wood unfurled, resin-scented, falling light as leaves from the sure-
passed plane- I pretended to ride inside the half-built vessel, waves
of imagination navigating the sea and, if not the sweep of the plane,
the swish of the cutting saw or the hammer of the hammer, then the
chonk-chonk of the cold chisel where he notched a beam that a beam
might grip.

Goggled like Barney Oldfield, my grandfather smoothed a metal fitting against a whirring stone wheel. It wasn't electric but powered
by a driving foot pedal like the New York City sharpener in Walt Whitman's poem, whose sparks shower the cosmos on an everyday street in
an ordinary neighborhood.

Honing an edge to fit exactly, caliper-gauged- it made for the
difference when a ship had to keep hitting its way through ocean waves,
taking the seas as they come, riding to crests, falling to troughs with
all the economy of an elegant structure designed to withstand the vast
rolling anarchy of a storm at sea.

When I watched him in his workshop, he built sea-worthy, fif-
ty-foot, fishing boats that he finished and sold one-by-one. I was a tyke,
four, five, six years-old. I only wish I had been old enough to understand exactly how he did it because building a ship, like building a
poem, is painstaking and complicated. First of all, it has to float.

Instead of driving nails, my grandfather preferred pegs. They gave. But, for bigger joints, steel plates with bolts spun by a wrench so big it nearly outweighed me. After I tried to lift it, I dropped it with a whang on the concrete.

He looked over, made sure I still had my fingers and both my feet, went back to the A-frame high above him while he guided an engine swung on thick chains into empty space between rising struts of the ship- as if he could do this day after day in his long working life. Then the noon whistle blew somewhere inside, and he walked with legs made of meat and potatoes into the house where my grandmother had laid out lunch on the dining room table.

By afternoon, when I returned from a nap, the westering sun of summer Los Angeles struck dusty side windows, divided into many squares and panes, and illuminated the shed where Jack built ships. The interior grew golden, and the ship's frame glowed at even-tide, ribs and beams lit-up in a world of Vermeer- as if light suffused from inside the wood and scattered tools, each object embodied with an aura of purpose and exactitude.

*

Too small to constantly watch,
they tied him to a mast below deck—
given the rise and dip.
the sideways pitch
in the North Atlantic—
so he wouldn't roll and crack his head.

Age four, Nils Jurgen Petersen
arrived at Ellis Island—
the customs man looked at his name and said:
"From now on, you're Jack."

    *

    Jack Sprat, Jack Shit, Jack be nimble,
    Jack be quick, Jack get up and get out of bed— you're
    ten years old in the New World, and you'll labor
    ten hours a day, six days a week
    for a dollar a day,

21

        the going wage
        on the Yellow Brick Road.

*

Looking through girders once, later through branches,
you catch the gestalt: a pattern that flips back and forth through ledgers,
ship masts, bone-pipe vests, double tracks: wagons gone west.

          *

        A church bell rings, but who's listening?
        The mail arrives at the wrong address.
        A knock on the door of the Philosopher's Club.
        When Bronson Alcott opens it, no one's there.
        Someone sighs because someone wept.
        It makes no sense: "Moose...Indian..."

*

A faded chart, shoals in the harbor, framed behind glass,
attached to a wall painted with fishes, draped with nautical net.
We sit, our drinks clink, but, fifty years ago, this watering hole
was out in the middle of the waves at Dana Point—
before they dropped the boulders,
built the breakwater, paved the cove.

The Pilgrim's log disappeared into an eastern archive,
and there's no navigational chart to find your way across this parking lot.
It's phantom fathoms where we sit, adrift on this limited premise.
Richard Henry once fished exactly here on his bumboat.

Stiff cowhides sailed from *ranchero* hands down the sandstone cliffs
to land on a deck, and the hides became, in time,
with a kiss of luck and a rounding of the horn,
American boots, belts, the binding on a book Thoreau read,
a cover for a chair where Dickinson sat,
looking out a window over Amherst.

Conversations are muted among the living, the dead.
A blind Gabrileño shaman sits in a distant past
where present lives test uncertain depths.
California, here I come! California, there you went.

*

In jack-light, Nils drifts out on the ebb tide
through walls and studs of the boat shed.
He's swinging a sledge to free the stays
and slide the ship along runners
down the driveway and into the river,
74th Street, just off San Pedro Boulevard.
Bound directly for the sea,
he's at the helm, a Viking
in denim overalls and a flat cap,
sailing past cars, trucks, buses.

I'm down in the hold, awash in the bilge,
half-light, deepest night, twilight.

I think we constellate our sea-bearings
by stringing stars on invisible threads,
slosh and roll, currents against the hull,
find our way home by reckoning.
Sea-shell to sailor's ear, you hear surf-echo,
sea-chantey, wave-dirge, child wail,
the mother in labor, the nurse saying, "There...there..."

            *

            Sails and trails on the whale's path,
            depths caught in tone-talk.

            I can hear Atlantic incisions
            carved in Pacific scrimshaw,
            the doomed Pequod, St. Elmo's fire
            dancing down the mast.

            Ahab!

            In a moment and forever, too,
            ghosts and their echoes
            feedback into loops—
            winds, runes.

Cleaning Woman

She was nothing more than a vacuum,
an emptied trash can, the office rug,
the shining waxed floor deepening the corridor
clarities of glass with lettered names,
important men who ran things.

She was mop, bucket, timecard per week
— don't tell me.

She rode the elevator down.
She rode the bus home.

*

Blackbirds on the window sill,
the widow sleeps in the kitchen,
slumped in her chair, barely
snoring, courting his visage.

She migrates through vague fields,
returns down the miles
of illusory grocery shelves,
bread boards, oven racks, race horses
to ride to put the platters under his nose.

Together they eat zeros.
Together they wrap up the fish
in The Wall Street Journal.

The floor gives way to a line of rocks
in the park where the old man used to stroll
and not once did he ever....

She sees a mountain range,
a blue valley rolling beyond.

Río

The San Gabriel was a southern California river—
a mile wide and an inch deep,
except those days when it really rained,
once or twice a year.
Then the beast awakened,
the dragon twisted and turned and roared
under highway bridges through the cities of the plain.

San Gabriel wasn't the first name.
The *Gabrieleño/Tongva* called it something before the Spanish arrived.
You would have to dig down through the sand, shake the word detritus,
sift through gravel layers before the invaders appeared.
You would have to privilege the first people
who scarcely were recognized or remembered,
yet one of them sat next to me in the third grade.

Manuel Bejarano's land was called *Shevaa*. It was beneath us,
and we wouldn't have dared pronounce the word,
much less envision a world where you might walk barefoot
along the water in the hot sand, pondering
houses woven from palm fronds under oaks,
dancers by fires, paths that meander, riddles without answers.

There's a shadow river, an undeniable river,
a river below of dreams and nightmares,
a river that wraps around and drags me downstream
through childhood in Whittier, the city beside the river,
a city named for a Quaker abolitionist—
it strains belief: John Greenleaf Whittier.
It was a city founded by Quakers
for a fireside poet of rural Pennsylvania ("Snowbound"),
a city with green lawns and fireplaces in a veritable desert.

There's a shadow world under this world.
The civilization brought with us was laid over it
like rolls of green sod rolled over the warriors
in the rows of white crosses. Sacrificial rituals
define the slasher flicks, and it's usually women

who are the victims. Outside the dance
in Palm Park, teenage boys who can't

are fighting again, punching, bleeding,
breathing hard, panting, swearing,
tearing the shirts off their backs,
going down in a tight embrace.

*

In Alta California, just above Baja,
we float in a cryptic current, an arid dream
with unknown calligraphy, sky-writing
woven in shifting cloud patterns— bird murmurations.

       Manuel— are you there in changing shapes?
       Or have you fled this desert? Yes,
       you and your people have been replaced.
       It's the northern European nocturne—
       torches bobbing to a jaunty leider
       while sirens converge on brush fires,
       Chicano uprisings on Whittier Blvd.

       The quail are quaking underfoot,
       ready to erupt in a rush and fly downwind.
       Sheriff deputies are loading shotguns,
       advancing in a line with raised night sticks
       against protest, against crowds gathering,
       against anything out of the ordinary.
       Shadows hide from copter patrol lights.
       They duck under the *manzanita*
       beneath sycamores and oaks,
       slipping into sidereal time
       so the star is still there, still shining
       despite whirlpools of dark matter.

       The world is lost to us,
       camouflaged, deceptive,
       divided by freeways,
       easily ignored when we're driving
       in streamlined steel and plastic,
       fast and oblivious.

Maybe he can somehow hear me,
that boy beside me in the third grade,
maybe if I whisper in the river of my sleep.

California Frontage

The repeated history of the eaves
explains the presence of the rains
and their relation to the leaves
in familial dining tables.

Strolling leisurely through the accounts
explorers create in these domains,
you can clearly see, through the walls,
how the vaults are full of holes,
the magazines surfeit with yearning.

In the distance, a necessary recess
glows dimmer and dimmer
as you tramp through the acceleration,
accoutrements deemed necessary
for ordinary behavior.

Amid the usual binge of subterfuge,
your tongue in the foreground talks in a flood
while the other within you
trusts in luck.

A map can only be accurate
with a bluebird on your shoulder.
It sings the truth, is gestural,
and all directions are dialectical.

*

We picked up a hitchhiker, a sailor in his Navy uniform who
was standing on the dark shoulder of the highway. My mother scooted
across the seat next to Evelyn after she opened the door, the interi-
or light came on, and the young sailor got in. During and just after
the Second World War, it was common practice to pick-up military
personnel. It must have been seen as part of a civilian's duty. Two,
young, pretty women answered a sailor's dream because as soon as he
got into the car and Evelyn pulled out on the road, everyone was laughing and talking back and forth in a fashion I hadn't seen or noticed before. I couldn't tell you what they said. The women might have started,

"Where are you stationed?" A frequent question in those years. And he might have said, "Oh, down in Long Beach. I'm on my way back from seeing my folks in Fresno. Where are you gals from?" I wouldn't have remembered the words or even the night if the young sailor hadn't placed his arm along the back of the front seat behind my mother. It awakened something within me, something that connected with my own burgeoning identity, and how that identity was inextricably connected with my mother and, quite probably, my missing father who was about to board a troop ship to return home, 1945. What was the stranger doing? Why was he doing this to my mother? She was mine, and I was hers. They laughed, talked, lit cigarettes and sang to the radio ("He's a boogie-woogie bugle boy from Company B...") along the Ridge Route in the immense darkness of night, the war, and lives in upheaval in a thousand and ten-thousand different ways- sometimes converging, sometimes departing, sometimes in a limbo of recognition and regret. I must have fallen asleep on the back seat, stretched out while we drove. Where did they drop off the sailor? Where did he go?

        *

        The years zip past
        like your address in the glass
        of a passing Cadillac,
        and the curbings repeat.

        The grass looks greener
        because it's older and well-kept
        women amble these avenues
        surrounded with leaves.

        Under the eaves of spreading ferns,
        we sit looking out for sunsets,
        flags by the driveways,
        cars returning from work,
        porches, doors, sunbursts in bas relief.
        We drift through windows by the sea
        and the saber-toothed fronds
        on the overhead palms
        rattle like fistfuls of keys.

Killing Floor

You toss the football in a spiral from far across the schoolyard.
I'm five or six, and it's coming in big, the yellow school bus.
My friend Tom asks the driver, who's leaving because he was drafted
to join the army and go to Korea, "Dan, will you bring me back a shotgun?"
Scattered in a pattern of misconceptions, Uncle Ott, who, my father jokes,
"is some sort of strange gauge, odd six or odd twelve,"
comes limping across the lawn, same year, at Sawtelle Veteran's Hospital,
all the way from the First World War, no *Arc d'Triompe*,
a bad leg, a bad hip, deep wounds and worse memories.
It was a hell of a trip to France, a hell of a sojourn in Paris.
Coming back to Cincinnati, he never married, but worked
much of his life in an Ohio River slaughterhouse,
Kentucky side, down on 'the killing floor.'
They sledged the steers in the head, slipped and slid,
five generations in the Deutsch ditch, stepped in it once, twice,
all their lives from Bull Run to just the other day among the Sumerians.
"They slit the steer's throat after they sledged it, see?"
The actual river runs outside because everything is fire.
The wells are burning, drop more bodies
into sand fires. "Eat, Hansel, eat!" The faster the
generations travel, the quicker the fire burns.
You can throw yourself out a window. You can stay
trapped inside, railroaded, staring out at dim vistas-
trenches for the young, slaughterhouses for maturity, veterans' hospitals
when you're done. Some just go numb in Covington.
Others whiff paint. Some pray, some scream, some claim
to see the face of Jesus in everything. but, amazingly,
nobody perceives anything. The classes ahead never look back.
Uncle Ott came walking across the lawn at Sawtelle,
having been through the war, having "won,"
and we sat on benches in the Los Angeles sun
under palms with some of his buddies
crudely tattooed by the usual fates-
a marmoreal dove impaled by a plunging dagger,
a secretary of war who waves to the corps
and a secretary of defense who waves from behind a fence.
"Keep the troops moving!" A constant ringing
shells the ears. In the darkness of the wards,

phantom limbs reach out windows of long-gone trains
to young lovers who have grown no older, who still smile
in dreams of deeply wounded veterans. In dreams at Sawtelle,
they crawl on their hands and knees through the offal,
slaughterhouses clogged with bodies. Sudden obstructions
appear to block the throats of once-bellowing steers,
while men under flares are lowing: "I'm not going!"
The flow over the top bogs down, the army falters.
Only the salon contains exquisite corpses,
only the parlor game remains playable at a secure distance
from history, The hospital becomes lost
in the smog of intersecting freeways. Values leap.
The property is worth more than the veterans. Their bones
must be burned in urns above the killing floor,
above the futures market, the stock market,
the bond market, the surplus stores.
How many fluctuations will it take to make a killing?
Private ashes, public ashes, further celebrations
of sacrifices in the wet muck that becomes the dead dust.
Oh, Otto, you had the kindest of smiles when
we met you on the lawn at Sawtelle.
You smiled your entire life, through it all,
through deceptive mazes, weirs, pens- the corrals laid out
in decreasing intakes to urge the stock forward
to the final line that leads onto the killing floor.
Otto, *sprechen sie, sprechen sie,* and check this-
I must have killed ten-thousand Germans
in war games, as a kid, before I realized
I was part-German, like you.
You were all German, all American, too.
You killed them, and they killed you.

Ornithology: A Rift

The visionaries dreamed sending rockets
through the shoulder of Orion,
a whirlwind of titanium to hit the Kremlin.
Huddled under school desks in the nuclear pretext—
we were kids at the vortex of binding energy—
scrapple from the apple.
Endless scroll print-outs from the computers
of exit velocities and re-entry equations
— the prose of the trans-Siberian express.
Death ships, cartoon strips, spontaneous bop prosody
inside a glass case in a museum of artifacts,
a poem on a pedestal—
"Run Over by an Inter Continental."
Suddenly, it was spacecraft and telemetry,
a moment when the soul arose
out of the mere body, fleeing earth
and all its bonds, liberated
from gravity and every one of its straps—
Transcendentalism once more!
All of it captured by cameras
with mad camera disease.
Cameras on cameras
(in case cameras deviate),
spy planes, satellite imagery—
the barely disguised desire to play God.
There's disease in a healthy body,
radiated rain on a sunny day. It's falling
in a colossal payback on our flattops,
boys in love with football, shotguns and Marines,
talking in tongues about God and Communism
swearing allegiance, pledging my love for thee.
Some whispered further confessions
before going back to reconsider
fast fish, loose fish, and fissures of men
broken-down, deranged with heat and friction
by re-entry equations in the night kitchen.

Factors of integrity grip the imagination.
Congress of birds—
so many places to run,
so few to hide from what flies overhead
somewhere in the blue, out of the blue.
"You'll pay for it, won't you?"

Three Streams

The eyewitness
said:

"First, there was light and
then came shock. The blast
wave shot across the open
water.

As the ship drifted
at the edge, as
we watched
the cloud rising
thousands of feet,
we removed
our goggles
and remarked on
the complete success—
thumbs up
from deck to deck.

Then the first sea birds
came flying toward us,
out of the cloud.
Their eyes had been burned
by the flash, the remains
drooled down their beaks.

In the screaming and
the circling, the circling.
and the screaming,

we met our surviving
witnesses, and we tried
not to listen
or see."

My mother said:

"My cousin Harriet told me
Klaus Fuchs was in
Clifton's Cafeteria, counting
the capital letters on the menu

because their number
is exactly the same
as the amount of uranium
he gave to Stalin."

[long pause]
"There is no menu
in Clifton's,"
my father said.
while my mother
passed him a dish.

"Yes," my mother said,
"that's why she goes there.
She can't read, you know.
She's retarded."

"She is?" I asked.
They looked at me, askance,
having forgotten my presence,
as we ate dinner, the
little face at plate level.

"Yes," my mother said.
"It happened
when she was born.
Uncle Harold was in
the Army in Texas,
and Aunt Mildred had her
on the stairs. They just
didn't deliver her right
in that Army hospital."

"It was a Naval hospital,"
my father said, correcting her.

Nobody said anything:

Lowering the boom, drilled
at school, we crouched
down under our desks

and tried not
to listen or see.

At home, at dawn,
when Dad and I watch
the Nevada test shot
live on TV, I want
to crawl behind the set,
get way back inside the
cabinet, out of sight
of the towering cloud
in the desert on the screen.

It seems the thing is
about to come through
the window and into
the room, just like the
night when the all-out
attack sirens went off
because of the rain,
and I was in bed,
thinking, "This is
the end, my friend, this
is the end…"

Later, I ask my father
to go over the signs
once more, the swipe
for a bunt, the swerve
for hitting away, curves.
where the cosmos warps,
time tears into uneven strips.

His cheek tics, the tea kettle
sings. Daylight is here,
but the night remains.

A Little Song for a Long Time Past

There's a place where I was raised, a town where the orange groves went down in the easter expansion of greater Los Angeles years ago. The wooden house of an old grower suddenly stood naked amid piles of uprooted trees. The piles were usually burned in the dawn while firemen in rubberized coats kept watch, drinking coffee and speaking sentences of steam as they leaned against the shiny red trucks. Huge yellow Cats came afterwards to turn the ashes into memories and cut the streets: one big furrow where there had been many little ones: field mice, jack rabbits and coveys of quail starting up from your feet in a rush. They always gave your heart a leap when you wandered those waist-deep grasses in spring, and the kid behind you ran all the way home screaming, "Snake!" Pickups arrived in the wake of the Cats, construction gangs layed down foundations and started nailing the houses in their rows. After they had all gone home, there were many times at dusk when we wandered through unfinished walls, studied rough plank floors below punched-out electrical circuit boxes and looked for slugs. Boulevards, signals, shopping center supermarket parking lots with scattered steel carts and canned music coming out of loudspeakers on light poles were soon to follow. On any evening there, you might have stepped out of your auto to hear A Hundred and One Strings play "The Orange Blossom Special."

*

Late summer nights in the seventies,
the windows wide open
and your slow boat rolling,
pitching down avenues to the beach,

redolent blossoms open perfectly
and you both glide,
reparian sailors beside the sea,
turning lovely curves along Jasmine Street.

Visionary Flight

Wallace Berman built a construction,
a cross with baroque ornamentation
said to include "obscene" imagery.

There was a trial. Kafka
was right. Berman was guilty of nothing
but insight, a revelation
of unusually juxtaposed emulsified emotion
      otherwise known as photo copy art
      — which, by the way, Berman invented.

    But he was found guilty
    by the court of Los Angeles County.

    It must have been subversive,
    secret with subtle rhymes
    such as the shape.
    The shape of Wallace's cross
    aped the shape of a secret
    high-altitude plane

    that was caught,
    taking pictures
    and then shot down
    over Russia.

    The pilot bailed out,
    Gary Powers.
    He was put on trial,
    found guilty, imprisoned,
    and later traded for a spy
    on the other side.

    He was a pilot who survived his ordeal,
    came home to be "an eye in the sky,"
    reporting traffic conditions
    from the Los Angeles heavens.

Nobody could change the verdict against Wallace Berman.
He was guilty of blasphemy, juxtaposing naked ladies
and religious icons. It was like the Sixth Patriarch
of Ch'an Buddhism who tore apart the scriptures. Wake up!
It was like Sinead O'Connnor ripping a picture of the Pope
on Saturday night truly alive— enlightening! In lightning!
Wallace Berman was guilty of high-altitude flying
and a low consensus with preying.

      He had been caught dancing on the wing
            with angels

              and other visions
                  seen in Semina

                      his magazine,
                        'the seed,'

                  visions of peyote,
                  of God and Gabriel

          trumpeting golden songs,
          flying above and ahead.

In this design, the cockpit is forward
of the wing juncture on the U-2,
much like the head of Jesus on the cross
with his arms outstretched,
a bird, a plane, an angel
dancing on a cloud
or nailed. It's a comedown.

Gary Powers crashed in the helicopter
and died in a heap of wreckage at a corner
in The City of the Angels— *Nuestra Señora,*
Our Lady of Sorrow.

Wallace Berman moved north to San Francisco.
I saw him in the Haight, cartoon night,
the Digger's basement on Page Street
— he was leaning against the wall,
a wise smile, outlier supreme
flying through the firmament. Later,
back on L.A., he was killed by a drunk driver
in Topanga Canyon— fire and gasoline.

Oral History: Talking in Our Sleep

The path leads across four lanes from the Hula Hut
over Whittier Boulevard to Pio Pico's adobe rancho,
the hacienda of last governor of the *Californios*,
and down toward the river, past the small rented house
where Alice lived, a girl I met at a matinee—
the first girl I really kissed seriously—
we made-out in the dark in the flickering flicks,
our tongues dancing. A strange beauty,
she was as skinny as I was, trembling, too.

In the night I move through the safe combinations
to make the tumblers click as they somersault
to reveal the papers and deeds. The river
runs wild over the banks and through the fields,
carrying away manuscripts and volumes
about the Spanish land grants.
Last-named after families,
we only know our first names.
"She's really Alicia," her friend tells me later.
It's a secret that doesn't matter to me.
Our tongues meet to talk in code. We speak
any language with smooth syntax.

This was my thought as I peered in the window
and saw Alice again, sitting beside her father on the couch,
his working class suspicions of me,
an interloper in the wrong neighborhood
who came to take his daughter on a date
in my friend's father's big sedan. Later,

I can't remember. It wasn't a house. It
was a prison of gender— my male gaze
reflected back from the glazed glass
as we watched the film at the drive-in,
the wars and the gun fights roaring
out of the little speaker on short leash—
the political leader who excused himself
to dump more bodies into the darkness beyond,

down the river, through the streets
and across the screens.

It wasn't a drive-in, it wasn't a movie.
It was a destination in the dark to kiss again,
to fall within and through the interstices
while the world went on with its time-clocks,
synchronized signals, stop signs, alerts,
and strands and strands— barbed wire
that wrapped around the Fred C. Nellis School for Boys,
the reformatory that was hidden by high fencing
down the boulevard of hope and try
with locks that locked-in steps
to ominous pipes and drums,
a marching corps that pranced
the delinquents toward responsibility.

It wasn't where I was going. We passed it by
without thinking, like the depots of weapons
further down the river at Seal Beach,
the buoys piled in their tiers,
the bunks where they cried at night,
as quietly as they could.

       Sand blew
       off the edge
       of the Rio Hondo.

       At the confluence,
       the deep background
       revealed everything.

       There were no escapes
       from the indoctrination
       that came with every commercial,
       with every lie about freedom
       and responsibility. I saw myself
       waving from the back
       of "Crow's Crutch,"

a black sedan hotrod
that a one-legged man
raced along the avenues,
a '34 Ford glossed
like obsidian rock,
streaking past,
my reflection again,
trying to catch Alice
as a real person, not
the product of my wishes,
not some far-off figure
floating down the river.

But we slipped in the current,
swept under the bridges,
washed down, out
into the ocean onto sandbars
in front of the Ray Bay power plant,
the ocean unnaturally warm,
a prescience of the future,
the need to cool the turbines
forever turning over the engines.

Where is Pico-Rivera? Where's
Downey? Artesia? I kissed
the back of her neck,
saying goodbye.
I am caught in a flick,
a moment in time, a tongue
across the river,
a low island in repose,
the grace and mystery
of a brown-eyed girl.
We are floating out to sea,
holding each other at midcentury.
She drifts away. I can't
reach her. We say,
"I'll see you soon."
"Sure as shooting"

We can't say help.
We talk in tongues.
It's godly, a language,
a prayer at the bed's edge
as we slide down night
into further depths.

Enforcement

A friend went full Chicano, dropped out
into the barrio, blond waterfall, lowered Chevy—
a portent of recognitions ahead— he was light years
in front of the rest of us, his fall
from status was either courageous
or lanquid acquiescence, bowing down
to the way of water
without resistance.
Maybe he was right.

In the barrio, Jimtown, the shacks sprawled
along the river— maids, gardeners— help
that wasn't allowed to live inside
Whittier's city limits. Once a week,
Jimtown's denizens
could swim in the city plunge— it was called
"International Day."
But who were the interlopers?
Who were the natives?

Who represented the best?
Who were the miscreants?

Some were in for extortion,
but not always the right ones.
Some were in for burglary
and crimes against property.
Some were in for Proudhon's thoughts,
some for grand theft— they lived rich
and storied, well-heeled and distinguished—
some were in grander theft,
and that's sublimely derivative.

A thousand business men bow their heads
at a prayer breakfast in the convention center,
and "a terrible beauty is born."

*

The patrol copter banks hard west and comes down
over a maze of odd curving avenues,
neons covered with vato spraygun logo whiz,
surf running miles in from the coast,
breaking away foundations and short-circuiting signals.

I repeat the codes on the static radio,
and we drone on in our glass fist,
hoping to find the usual rows
of whitewashed, look-alike houses in the sunset.

The word comes back that the beasts of the elfin forest are free,
thieves with balloon pockets and no morality
who pour sand down oil shafts and stack orange crates
to make wobbly ladders up to your bedroom window.

Then we look down and spot the oaks stepping into the avenues,
dancing with the sycamores— European "plane" trees—
and the oleander spilling out from the center medians
to grow over the shoulders and vanquish the roads.

It's reported that mowers have escaped from garages
to run up and down carpeted halls,
and wild bulldozers cut blithe intaglios
all over once-smooth parking lots.

*

Full of dead good
and good and dead intentions.
So much stone broken
into glass, and glass into sand.

"Was I cut out for this?"
a voice inside asks
to no one who can answer.

Wash the window,
raise the blind to lower again.

Sand into fire,
rain into fire and wind.

We are born into them—
into broken lives,
into broken times

Ode to Internal Combustion

Machines leaped from the line. The starter was up and down, up and down. Terry kept trying to explain why he had to marry Lynn. He was pie-eyed and he'd been crying and his head was down. It was hard to hear his words between the burning slicks and the engine screams because we were parked too close to the pits. Sharp sat low in the back seat, tapping his fingernails in changing rhythms on the top of his beer can, and I had the spins. I leaned forward on the dash, trying to listen to Terry and trying not to. It was the first time I'd ever been truly drunk, and I didn't know where I was headed except that I thought I was going to be sick because I couldn't keep back the saliva in my mouth.

"Well," Sharp said, "You might do worse— she's a fine girl."
Terry said yeah, but his voice cracked.
"Geez, man, I'm only sixteen..."

I had just looked up from the dash to see a modified Ford coupe fishtail hafway down the strip. It never caught traction and the skid drowned Terry's words as the rod spun and slid off the asphalt into the dirt, flipped on its side and flamed-out in the darkness.

The fire engine and the ambulance came careening from behind the bleachers, and I opened the door, leaned out and heaved.
Later, we heard that there were only minor injuries.

*

When I was a child, I watched my mother smoke
and talk on the phone.
The Russian was about to bang his shoe
on the United Nations podium.
For your birthday, I promise not to bury you.
I'll bring you a drip hovering in midair
from the hand of the man born in Cody, Wyoming—
who attended Manual Arts
while my parents grew up at the same time in Los Angeles.
Jackson Pollock went east and became a legend.
Success in those years meant
driving an Oldsmobile, and he did— straight into a tree at ninety.
But so did my Dad. Well, he didn't hit a tree head-on.
He rolled his Olds.

He thought it was a cat that ran right out in the road.
He had to swerve. Or
it was a rabbit that night— darted in front of him
from an avocado grove.
He wasn't sure. He didn't really remember,
he said with a shrug.
My mother cast a cold eye on the cat and/or the rabbit.
We were visiting him in the hospital, and she said, "I just bet".

*

We roamed the drive-in flicks
below the gun fighters and bright breasts
— monumental technisexual magnificence.

We laughed as we stole hubcaps
and sucked gasoline through siphons.
We were princes of porcupine hair
who frenched the air with our fists.

We were young and infamous
on the boulevards of gas
where grown men
tripped their tongues
with talk of torque

but still had to lie
beside their wives
in television ghost night,
and I saw our time
tuned to the timing light.

Ratchet be thy name,
socket wrench thy fate.

All the machinery was
caressed vividly
when I was
young and uneasy
under the freeway.

                            *

There were days driving down Whittier Boulevard when I looked out through windshields and saw the distances along the lanes and onto the horizon that sent my heart longing for an escape. It was the same great pull of the frontier that is forever behind every American headed west and far into a future we eternally invent, an improvised projection that takes us out of the past and its tired tyrannies. Immigrants. We're headed for coasts and islands, continents beyond, crossing oceans and seas, sailing through sunsets into destinies that we can't begin to understand in all their complex imperial design. It's as if we wished to be innocent travellers, pilgrims who had no responsibilities for the stamps in their passports, for the people who served us, who protected us. Even in our joyous music and dancing, the purest arts, direct connections with the body and emotions, we were beneficiaries of traditions that went back through Native America and Africa as well as European folk. The road beckoned, the engine fired, someone policed the traffic, timed the signals, constructed the entire shebang, and, yet, we imagined it was our own initiative and actions that were entirely responsible for everything.

*

Behind the beaches, the plains
cut back into the red ocher,
yellow ocher canyons.
On the flats, the Torrey pines
have been slashed to the quick
to lift houses on pads,
where rainbirds turn circles
through grasses and ornamentals.

Beyond, sage, coyote bush
and the elfin forest survive drought years
when rabbits come at dawn—
graze fresh-watered lawns.

Where the freeway cuts and concretes the access,
animals are funneled through the underpass.
Nights in your lights
(maybe one-eyed, returning from parties)
their eyes flash and they move hugely
into a suddenly new view.

But they pass as fast as a pair of hips
in a party kitchen
moves behind you, brushing you, lightly
inscribing a small intaglio in your imago,

a moment between car and animal,
between hello and where are we going to go?

The onramp beckons, the empty lanes
bridge the dry streams, the old water courses
where animals are found in dreams,
a passing fancy of endless party people
dancing in circles, wanting...

The animals are wanting. One half
of our face caves away. We stand,
along the chain-link, waiting
to cross the impassable highway.

Out on the Playground

Someone showed
how you could fold
George Washington's head
and make
a mushroom
cloud out of
a dollar
bill. Or
a circum-
sized cock.

"What the fuck!"

It appears God wanted to toss
human fate across the cosmos
with a spotless pair of dice.

"In California, my mother said she went to the store,
and all the shelves were empty
because of the coming war."

On an Indian summer
weekend in New England,

the first leaves fell
from northern limbs—
maples and birches.

The first toadstools
thought about coming up

in the ring of leaves
around each tree.

"In a nuclear age, nations
wage war as porcupines make love—
cautiously."

Tiny planes,
blips on screens,
dishes turning.

On a long table in a big casino,
gleaming like the open sea,

across the maps,
symbols of ships
moved by a croupier
to arrange the coming
confrontation
in the War Room.

The War Room— where they move
flags over charts, fire in the hole,
as the munitions business booms.

On October 26, the FBI reported the Soviet embassy torched
their archives, the last diplomatic act
in preparation for war.

About Black Saturday in particular,
about the entire Cuban Crisis, Khrushchev said:

"A smell of burning hung in the air."

Waves are Ghosts of Storms Across the Ocean

From the hills of Montezuma
to the shores of San Clemente
I was in the surf at Church,
listening to long range artillery
— Marines on maneuvers
in the hills of Camp Pendleton
preparing for the next one—
distant thunder— a roar in a shell—
jarheads headed for hell
— poor kids, just my age
when I rode waves.

*

They called that surf break "Church" because there was a small chapel of corrugated steel siding and a similar steel roof that the Marine Corps had built for the troops during the Second World War. The little church stood just above the beach, framed by a couple of palm trees (*Washingtonia filifera*, the palm native to southern California, as old as dinosaurs, birds and crickets). When I floated out in the break between sets of waves, I'd often wonder about the services inside that church for the young men who were soon to head west, 1942-1945, cross the Pacific and storm those palm-fringed, coral beaches on the atoll islands where the Japanese waited. It was the same year I was born, so, like everyone in America, We owed those boys more than prayers and wishes to any god could ever give. I could understand their fear before shipping-out, although nobody could estimate the coming terror they faced.

*

My 8th grade teacher,
a man from Terre Haute,
read to us one day a story
about his time on Guadalcanal.

The enemy lurked all night in shadows
at the edges of the clearing. In the flares,
figures seemed to be darting.
Shouts, cries, bursts of shooting,

but it turned out to be nothing,
a night when nothing happened-
this made it more frightening.

The big hair of the tough girl
with the sharp mouth
who sat behind me
brushed my shoulder,
touched my sleeve
as she laid her cheek
on her arms on the desk
in order to hide from it.

Photos of family faces
appeared and disappeared
in the broad leaves.
Bodies in camouflage
washed up on curbs
in dreams of suburbs,
liana vines wound
through attic rafters,
blue trumpet flowers
floated in radio waves.
Rivets from warplant wings
had been brought home
to help hold a cracked
plaster ceiling, a literal map, a
seismograph of earthquakes, wars-
structural faults that sent things flying.

In the years after the war
before the next war
through the aisles of surplus stores,
we ran past overstock, remains,
trying to make the loud sounds of guns,
childish tongues, dumb kids
who believed helmet liners were really helmets,
not knowing how heavy the real thing was.

Commuter

"My shoulder still bothers me,"
he said, of a wreck he failed to preface.
You were always coming in on the middle of film *noir*
merely by living in southern California after the last war
during the present war and before the next war.

Divorced, he became obsessively ordered.
The car, the gun, the glasses were always clean.
The rug required straightening every few minutes
between another glug and another rail
about the requirements of punishment for
"anyone who got out of line."

Passing a location, a smash at an intersection in time,
a broadside, the gap was wide. Fiery bodies inside.
Driving through the oil wells at sunset,
you barely noticed the waves of fins,
chrome streaks as they came and went.

He peed in his bathroom sink
"because the toilet bowl splatters," he explained.
Then he would wash his teeth, being quite careful,
to avoid cavities, in the sink where he had peed.

Sitting in the driver's seat, morning after morning,
an empty tree of routes in the head,
knowing each avenue and thus making it all
impossible to forget, the life of a commuter
beckoned like a pistol at the neck,
or the small satisfaction- having a run of signals click.

He fucked a woman down the street
by first making love to her
and then telling her husband.

At the peak of prosperity in this realm of destiny,
it was enough to buy a lot for once,
the purchase of which, conditioned by the cliff,

slipped ever downward as the land did,
each new depression giving rise to the next.

He died, hating life,
this working-class uncle of mine,
but, as someone in the family said,
trying their hardest to redeem,
"He was always neat and clean."

Funneled through an underpass
in a dream of decades passing,
one will see, as many men and women did,
the unrelieved monotony of the prospects.

War Poems

Out at the end of the runway,
they dump the scrapped choppers
shipped home from the war.

The west wind comes up every afternoon.
Crash-twisted rotors creak and scrape.
On some wrecks, the hinges are bad.
They squeak and cry.
The junk's hold on reality: tenuous, at best.
Large black spiders run across the metal.
"Able One, this is Delta Triangle."

*

On Iron Mountain, passing clouds,
loud falls and deep drum rolls:
rocks, tumbling in the strong current,
run over rocks trying to hang on.

On Iron Mountain, they sneak a peek
in the middle of the prayer
and fall in love again with their wingtips.

The wingtips glisten under the glittering lights
because the polish is so high.
They shine like rivers far below.
They shine like John Wayne's eyes
when he relented just a little.

*

When you came before the Khmer Rouge,
they asked to see your hands.
If you wore eye-glasses,
you were a fascist, and they shot you.

If you didn't wear glasses,
but you lacked callouses on your hands,
you were a fascist, and they shot you.

In the 1870s in France,
the government troops in Paris asked to see your hands.
If your hands had callouses,
you were surely a communard,
and they shot you.

*

Los Angeles- 1949- the fire escapes
were hot, the troop parades loud
on Pacific Boulevard. Planes flew in formations
through our brains. When my red-haired uncle
came back from the veteran's hospital,
his hair was white.

San Francisco, 1969- people in the streets
marching against the war;
cops charging us, rushing
with raised clubs. In the chaos
I nearly went down: a provocateur at my back
kicked me in the heel
with his steel-toed boot.

That July, I was going to a meeting
of conscientious objectors. "What a knucklehead,"
my father said. The streets were deserted:
no one else arrived. They had all stayed home
to see the landing on the moon.

A woman I met years later
told me it was the first night she made love.
Everyone inside, in front of their sets,
waiting to take the first, weightless step.

Struggle

Sirens of war pulse,
the roof falls in
on the terrorized bull.
Light bulbs explode.

The sorrows are black,
the constabulary white.
Night falls, billy clubs
sweep the streets.
Skulls ring.

In the American labyrinth,
we wake up in limbo
doing the shuffle,
the living and the dead,
events and their echoes.

*

After they pulled us over with flashing red lights, the two L.A. cops told us to get out of the car. Then they threw Bob and me against the hood because we were headed down Central Avenue to hear Miles at the It Club. They didn't like white boys mixing with the locals in the ghetto. They wanted to know if we were "hopheads," too, so they could "bust you good." But we were just kids getting shoved and slapped by a couple of red-faced enforcers of the law. It got them off.

Tough guys love feeling powerful, and they probably laughed when they sat back down in their prowl car because we were scared to death and promised them we were going straight home. Underneath it all, they were scared, too. The macho myth is the worst thing "real men" ever talk themselves into. Many never find their way out of that maze.

"The essential American soul is hard, isolate, stoic, and a killer. It has never yet melted." D.H. Lawrence wrote this thought at a ranch in the mountains outside Taos, New Mexico as part of his book, *Studies in Classic American Literature.* Even though Lawrence is delivering a sweeping generalization one-hundred years ago, 1922, the sentence underscores American culture. Americans became brutalized by frontier genocide and the frontier's absence of women, by southern slavery, and the history of the denigration of labor in this country. You see violence flare and erupt in the revenge for Custer's Last Stand when the American Army massacred the Sioux at Wounded Knee for the "crime" of resistance, the Ghost Dance religion, and in the western campaigns against many other indigenous tribes— not to mention the post-frontier concentration camps (or reservations), the enforced agriculture and schooling and suppression of langauges and cultures. Demanding a monoculture out of rich diversity is exactly the problem of internal and external imperialism. You see Lawrence's exposé of our violence expressed by U.S. foreign wars and actions against nations across the world. Every mass shooter in America aspires to be the hard isolato, even as they are mostly opposite types— haunted by their own inadequacies.

This is the American labyrinth, the American conundrum—heroes won't be defeated, their souls don't melt. Ice-cold realists: rock hard, dependable. Terse with tough guy talk, machine gun dialogue. The tone of how many manly novels? Yet, late in the American night, there are many frightened, trembling human beings, fragile souls who've grown sick from the killing.

*

Tract houses go up on one side
of a *Diebenkorn* street,

— lyrical waves of light in
the wide-open spaces of California,
blue minds by the blue sea—

oil derricks and defense plants
fall away on the other.
Crossing the sky,
vanishing trails
define the *zeit*.

*

My cousin Jack's pumping regular in an L. A. gas station when a bum walks up and tugs on Jack's sleeve, a beat-down wino begging for money. Jack turns and looks at him, looks again. "Geez," he tells me, "it's none other than our Uncle Donald, who's living in the streets, asking for a handout."

Flabbergasted, Jack takes him home, has to rip off Donald's dirty, tattered, stinking clothes, puts him in the bathtub while Donald weeps in shame.

Before work the next day, Jack leaves Donald table money. When he returns home, late afternoon, long light down the boulevards, the money's gone. So's Don.

Nobody in the family ever sees him again.

*

Cross-eyed, he was teased as a child, stuttered.
Pre World-War II, he enlisted in the Army—
sent to Scofield Barracks in Hawaii
"They treated him terribly," my aunt said.
"His sergeant beat him every day."
He washed-out of the Army, came home,
couldn't support his first wife,
did roofing, construction,
spent nights in bars,
slept in a backroom at my grandparents.
He started falling drunk in the streets,
lost his rudder, drifting to skid row,
ended-up in the gutter.

It was months before the proper authorities
relayed an official letter to his sister (my mother).
In effect, he could not cash any more checks
since he was already X.

Thus, this notice was the only condolence
and the surf broke over our heads.

Coda

The river flows straight, the river twists
and doubles back— a sidewinder's path in sand.
The river contains the Milky Way,
a recognizable map of the region.
The ground painting's the remnant of the vision conveyed,
the course the water ran, when it ran,
as the poem is a remnant, a scrap from the whole whorl.
The songs that explained this cosmos have been lost,
the painters long gone. Only the vision remains.
One defined circle overlays another,
a world of interactive realms:
the world above and the world below,
roots and branches, sparkling water and burning stars.

Outside Katcha and Amu, what we call Orion and the Pleiades,
an oceanic line, a circle, defines the inner holdings: earth and sky.
The ring also delineates the coastline.
Far beyond the end of the river,
the dots off the edge are literally offshore islands.
The water is turquoise there, and, once, on a small boat,
we nearly drifted close enough to touch one of those islands.

Down in the clear depths where silver fish
swam through the ribs— a wrecked ship—
we may have glimpsed a catalyst,
as the Indigenous clearly did, a catalyst
to set the mind adrift in a perceptive sea.

*

The river flows temporal and eternal

through finite time and infinite space.

History is a nightmare I am trying to elucidate.

*

I'd like to compare an Appalachian singer who thrills, even chills,
with a high, pure keen, but not to this stream.
Cutting rock longer
than you'd care to remember, it was rippling
before it was dreamed.
You can't gauge it. Charts we've made find no moraine,
no certain flow that goes from peak to sea,
to say nothing of its aching cold,

or how sweet it might taste
if we could partake.

Partake?

Slake your thirst, stranger,
drink deep, ponder gratefully.

Dangerous Ideas

Dangerous Ideas

*"The rocks are ringing— they are ringing
in the mountains."*

Port of San Antonio, Texas
Sept. 21, 1889

Only the canvas-covered book has any special history, the book with the bullet hole in it. It was, or rather the pictures were, drawn by a Northern Cheyenne Indian while in confinement at Fort Robinson, Nebraska during the winter of '78, '79. I was Post Adjutant. I endeavored to get the book but its owner and maker refused to part with it for any price. So I gave the matter up. It purports to depict the deeds of several of the Northern Cheyenne during their famous march from Indian Territory [Oklahoma] to Wyoming Territory. The outbreak of the Cheyennes is well known, and as a consequence of the outbreak, I got the book in this manner. Four troops commanded by Captain Wessels, who by the way, was severely wounded, surrounded the hostiles and charged upon them killing all the bucks and unfortunately in the melee, some woman and children, but previous to the charge I saw an Indian with the book pressed down between his naked skin and a strap around his waist; another strap went between the middle of the book and around his shoulder. I turned to Private Laselle of H troop who was near me and said, "I want that book if we come out all right." Several others of the enlisted men heard me also. When the fight was over, and as the dead Indians were being pulled out of the rifle pit, they drew out finally my Indian with the book, apparently dead; the book was injured to the extent of a carbine ball through it and more or less covered with fresh blood. This fight took place near Bluff Station, Wyoming Territory, January 22, 1879. This fight was the closing one of a series of fights with the Indians, and they perished to a man.

In haste,

Frank

*

In early November, 1889, Black Sharp Nose, Grasshopper, and Porcupine left Tongue River Reservation without permission and rode in secrecy to a destination three hundred miles south in Wyoming. A similar party of Sioux from the Pine Ridge Agency in South Dakota rode west with three horses each, bundles of dried food and wire cutters. Ranches had spread across the northern plains and the Sioux cut their way through fences as they skirted houses and settlements.

When the various tribal groups gathered at the common destination, the reservation of the Wind River Arapahoe at Fort Washakie, they spoke of one thing: the Messiah in the far west. Among the tribal people, a delegation was chosen to travel, find this man and learn of the new belief. The delegation, Porcupine among them, left Fort Washakie and rode south to the Union Pacific line.

Twenty years earlier, at Plum Creek, Nebraska. Porcupine had been a band of Northern Cheyenne who had successfully attacked a railroad train— one of the very few times this happened. They derailed the engine, opened the box cars, rode their ponies across the plains with bolts of calico tied to the pony tails, unwinding an American skein while the boxcars burned behind them across the plain in the night.

Later, the railroads made a deal with the tribal people: if they let the trains have right of passage, the Indigenous could ride on the top of the cars.

*

At first light, a stiff, morning plains wind
wraps the batten board station, Rawlins, Wyoming,
flaps the close-drawn blankets and robes,
the row of figures who sit atop the cars
against the early sky. From their vantage,
they look ahead through
the wispy steam of the locomotive,
elk horns mounted on the light cowling,
and they see little streams of dust running
the gleaming steel rails headed west.
Somewhere between Ahab and Bartleby,
between the obsessive quest, manifest destiny,

the conquest of the lands of tribal people,
that vast sea of prairie and plains,
and the helpless slide of the writer
who only copies, staring at the brick wall,
a slide into passive resistance, coffins glided
on parallel tracks with daft purposes
assured by their solemn bearing—
boxcars full of buffalo hunters
whose spits in the wind corrected windage.

32,000,000 pounds of buffalo bones
shuffled east on the shuttling freight trains
looming cyclopean in the warp of our night,
32,000,000 pounds of bones for everything
from buttons to fertilizer. The hides
became the first conveyor belts
while the meat rotted along the ties,
and didn't those buffalo eyes shine in the moonlight
like thousands of nickels in a world without flies?

*

On June 15, 1890, the Northern Cheyenne file into a room at Camp Crook, seating themselves in a row of chairs before the desk of Major Carroll. Black Sharp Nose, Grasshopper, and Porcupine already sit in chairs beside the Major's desk. When the officer asks Porcupine to tell of the trip west since people in Washington have an interest, the man nods, starts to talk, the interpreter follows, and the commander's pen scratches across the sentences. For an hour, as the pen returns to the well and the pages turn, Porcupine describes how they sat atop the cars for the train travel of a thousand miles, the gathering of many tribes to follow the Messiah in Nevada.

When Porcupine first mentions this man, who he only refers to as Christ, all the Cheyenne take off their hats and the Major duly notes it in brackets.

In six months, hundreds of Sioux Ghost Dancers will be massacred in the snow at Wounded Knee, but, for now, the miracles are recounted, the Major's pen marks its tracks, a breeze stirs through the open window, and a meadowlark sings in Montana.

*

Crow Woman's Song

One good American cow
One good well-broken pair of oxen
Came walking across the water
Led by the soldiers

In the distance
On the other shore

I saw my children
Dancing

I went dancing
With my dead children

*

"April 16, 1900: Porcupine, chief ghost dance medicine man of the Northern Cheyenne, was, with Crook, White and Howling Wolf, on the Upper Tongue River, making medicine."

*

June 8, 1900. "I am still of the opinion that the best interests of the Northern Cheyenne and the service would be subserved by the removal of at least Porcupine and Crook from the reserve and their being held in custody until such time as they are thoroughly cured of their dangerous ideas. This man Porcupine is a smooth talker and a cunning Indian."

*

Being taken away for a year-and-a half of hard labor
among the Christian folk at Fort Keough
for their "dangerous ideas,"

Crook and Porcupine—
two fifty-year-old men in frayed buffalo robes
sat back-to-back in chains
in an open wagon in the American rain.

Welcome to the twentieth century!

*

In 1893, after James Mooney had visited Wovoka, J. I. Wilson— the Messiah's white stepbrother by adoption— obtained permission from the government to take Wovoka to the World's Fair in Chicago. J. I. figured that Wovoka's fame would make him an attraction and the venture would be a profitable one. But a month before the two men were to depart, Wovoka went up into the hills and stayed in hiding for 8 weeks, or until all thought of the journey had been abandoned.

*

Chicago, 1893

Frederick Jackson Turner is presenting his American Frontier Thesis when a hand is raised from the back of the hall and a tall Indigenous man in a black beaverskin hat stands up to interrupt the proceedings.

"It was quite unprecedented," a respectable professor of American History remarked later. "We were in the midst of absorbing Turner's ideas on the frontier, how it distinguished America from Europe, how it created democracy and equality, and why it was the central fact in American history and experience, when this Indian had the audacity to interrupt our learned proceedings…"

*

Wovoka laughs and holds up a strand of barbed wire in one hand.
Then he circles the strand around his neck. He laughs again,
and from his pocket he takes a small telescope, opening it outward
but holding it the wrong way— with the large end of the instrument
to his eye, and the small end to the audience and to Jackson Turner
up at the dais, mouth agape. Collapsing the telescope
he returns it to his pocket, and then removes his hat, releasing
thick, black braids that fall to his shoulders. Then he holds the hat
so that the audience might look inside the crown. What do they see?
What did they ever see?

*

If Jack Wilson was made aware of European traditions
by his adopting family,
who read him the Bible, and Porcupine's wife, Weasel Woman,

aka Angela, the German immigrant child taken captive
by the Northern Cheyenne from a ranch in Kansas,
was made aware of Indigenous traditions by her adopting family,
this universe expands in opposite directions, parallel and telling,
but always moving between a postcard of the Ghost Dance Messiah
standing on a Nevada street corner in front of a movie theater,
staring into the camera, 1915, and this Northern Cheyenne woman
photographed by a ceremonial fire in a *tipi* in the 1920s
     — gray hair in Heidi braids—
smiling with delight, saying "Ja" for years,
wandering with the tribe in the wilderness.

*

Technical director on a western film being shot in the Owens Valley near Lone Pine, California in 1924, Colonel Tim McCoy (the former adjutant-general of the territory of Wyoming and the future cowboy actor and early television host of an afternoon kids program I watched in Los Angeles in the 1950s) was interested to hear that the legendary Ghost Dance messiah was still alive— living beyond the White Mountains near the town on Yerington, Nevada. On a Saturday, McCoy borrowed a company car and drove across the state line. Directed to a ramshackle house in Yerington, McCoy knocked on the door, spoke with a young Paiute man who knew English and then encountered a heavy-set, sad-looking older man in a black beaverskin hat, dark vest and suit, with cowboy boots— the Ghost Dance originator.

Wovoka spoke in Paiute, a Shoshonean tongue, through the young man, his nephew, who, in turn, translated back and forth. The old man knew English but only conversed with McCoy in this fashion, a process that was extenuated by the Paiute tradition of translation that involved a repetition of the initial language by the translator's repeat of it again before any translation was made, and the same process from the translator when McCoy replied or asked a question. McCoy expresses impatience with this process in his written remembrance of the encounter.

However, one can see that this method encouraged the learning of each language in the translation process by everyone involved. But McCoy was in a hurry to return to his duties on the film and so he invited Wovoka to ride to Owens Valley with him for dinner and to meet some of the Native American extras on the film, including

Short Bull, a Sioux medicine man, another Sioux, Kicking Bear, and the Arapahos— Goes-in-Lodge and Yellow Calf— all of whom had visited the Messiah in 1889 when the Plains Indians travelled by rail to western Nevada and Wovoka had "died" in front of them—his heart no longer beating— until he returned again and told them of his vision of a cloud that was coming to envelop the white man. However Wovoka refused McCoy's offer, saying he would only come to meet the extras on the film if McCoy sent a car the following day. This demand struck McCoy as excessive, but he eventually agreed. Accompanied by his nephew, Wovoka was driven over to the Owens Valley the following afternoon for dinner with the film crew and the extras. The dinner might have made a curiously interesting film in itself, but no one thought to roll the cameras. McCoy says that none of the Arapahos or Sioux would look Wovoka in the eye, and the messiah never removed his hat— which, in the past he had done on occasion before his assembled followers who swore that he showed them the new world coming inside the crown.

    *

When he takes off the hat, we see far into the visionary's mind,
this hat full of the new world coming inside.
The land flows over the brim, the valleys run deep
north and south of Walker Lake with its blue expanse
below the 11,000 foot high sacred mountain
where the Numu world began.

When he takes off his hat, rising sage plains extend up alluvials
and into the foothill forests of his speech.
Is that snow bannering
off the highest peaks or just a reflection of the aura
of the visionary?

The central ceremony, the all-night trance dancing,
was accompanied by songs:

> "The wind, the whirling wind,
> turns the little flowers around and around.

> The rocks begin to ring.
> They are ringing in the mountains."

Now the scholars turn over the accounts
and inspect the entrances and exits.
A little cloud drifts across the mountains
and rains on a small circle of listeners.

The hat goes back on his head. The dancers rise up in songs.
Decades pass. Flamingos, cormorants, pelicans and grebes
fly the fossil flyway on rock walls
from an age when the Caribbean connected with the Pacific.

And yet their descendants still soar today.
Up the road in a stream-fed canyon,
native palms carry the scent of orange blossoms
as if they knew for a million centuries what was to come
while the wind and the birds repeat what is past to come,
turning and turning with the dancers in the dawn.
Year by year, era by era, eon by eon,
rains-sand-winds hone mountains to kingdoms gone.

*

History among ghosts—
who's to say A'piatan's wrong?

He thought Wovoka was a fraud
after a long trip on the Union Pacific.

*

After he was too old to work on the ranches or to climb up into
the ranges to fall timber, he walked the long, sage valleys across the bottom of ancient Lake Lahonton, hunted rabbits and watched cars plume
dust on roads far in the distance.

Hunting rabbits— that was how James Mooney first encountered Wovoka: Six feet tall, heavily framed, cradling a rifle in the pale,
December sun of Nevada. Thicker framed in later years, he was bent by
the weight of his single son's death as a child— the baby he played with
and delighted in when Mooney finally reached the wiki-up on New
Year's Night in the snow of 1892— the year the ethnologist traveled
32,000 miles in search of the ghost.

When Wovoka died in the early 1930s, a series of letters he had received between 1908 and 1911 were discovered in the basement of the Wilson house. Sent from reservations in the West and Canada, the letters carried news of recent sicknesses and troubles, with requests for red ocher and feathers to bring the dying back to health. The last of these letters, the only one that's typewritten, came from across the border in California.

*

Mr. Jack Wilson
Yerington, Nevada
Dear Jack,

How are all the Indians getting along down there? Please write and tell me. I heard lots of Indians died down to Yerington lately. Is this so? We are all well here. There is about four feet of snow in Bridgeport. At Uncle Tom's place there is about seven feet of snow. The Indians can't get out, and they're hungry. Tom's folks are all well only they can't get much to eat. Old Man John Craig has been down to Mono Lake and there has been so much snow he did not come back yet.

We all send our kindest regards and hope you'll write again soon.

Daisey Bell

*

He told Clare Chennault and the other pilots he was Panamanian, and that was fine with them. If he had told them the truth, they wouldn't have let him pilot one of the planes. He was half-white. That was all right, but he was also Numu Paiute, born in Nevada. That would be wrong because everyone knew Native Americans couldn't fly planes. Not that it mattered. He flew well and shot down several Japanese planes before he was shot down himself, lost somewhere in China, presumed dead, his grave never found.

Randomly picking up a book about the Flying Tigers in a small community college library in Coos Bay, Oregon where I taught in the spring of 1988, I learned about this American. I had taught in China the year before and traveled to Kunming during the Chinese New Year celebration. This is where the Fying Tigers had their base in the Second World War. If I'd known then, I might have even tried to find this lost pilot's grave. But, given war's vagaries, there may be no grave. He was Wovoka's grandson— born in a box car in Nevada.

*

In the late afternoon my family and I parked across the highway from the boarded-up train stop at Wabuska, Nevada, outside Yerington, where the Plains Indians got off the train from Wyoming when they came to see Wovoka in 1889. There was a rundown tavern, and we went inside. We ordered two beers and a coke for the kid while I asked the old woman bartender, in the wooden tavern-on the-lean, and the only other customer, an equally old man, about the Numu Paiutes of the area. They were telling me about the relations between the white ranchers and the local tribe when a Nevada highway patrolman swaggered in and demanded to know why the two semi rigs, loaded with feed lot cattle, were parked on the shoulder near the tracks across the highway and who the drivers were, and where they were, too. We all shrugged, but I had seen the drivers when we pulled up. Two long-haired Indigenous young men in cowboy clothes, headbands around their long hair.. They evidently left the trucks running and disappeared. Maybe the young men had gone up in the mothership, maybe they had wandered away into the vast desert. Maybe they decided that the life of a truck driver taking cattle to slaughter wasn't worth it and rode away with someone else. In the worse case, someone kidnapped them to hijack the beef. The dilemma upset the patrolman. He demanded our IDs as if we had something to do with it. I guess we did— just being there a hundred years later.

We were a century late and missed out on the miracles. We'll never see them, but the eyewitnesses at that time said they did. That's about the best answer I can give to the enigma of a Messiah and a crisis cult born of genocide and concentration camps. If you want an answer to any of it, recall the words of James Mooney who came in the wake of the Ghost Dance and wrote the voluminous report on the Ghost Dance for the Bureau of American Ethnology. Searching the same area for Wovoka in the 1890s, he describes arriving at night and driving around in a fog in the desert, "circling to no purpose on a wagon in the sage and calling out in the hope of hearing an answering cry."

*

A Song You Can't Sing

The conquered were swirled,
swallowed in Orion's deep nebula, cold fire,
while we rocked on the veranda,
the old homestead, locked inside
a house made of bottles.

From the lackadaisical roof to the bison hoof,
we never gave up our received attitudes,
slinking mountainous latitudes,
our serious summits where we
planted our flag, predators prancing
with indigenous scalps.

We drove forever west to bunk with drunken bugles,
and sang to the tune of "Garry Owen,"
"The Girl I Left Behind."
As November sings to October,
so many golden aspen leaves sent swirling
into fading memory
east of the mountains—
cultures, languages, ways of life
gone downstream in time,
only to be swept up by avid anthropology
busy as bees at the museum hive.

Euros privilege stone and marble monuments,
memorials to their belief in eternity,
their everlasting lives.
Those outside this vertical mindlessness—
the enslaved, who had next-to-nothing,
the very poor, because they couldn't afford it,
the Indigenous, who lived in a world beyond,
undefined space as opposed to regulated time.
There's this adamantine problem of property,
the dilemma of lines, the orderly accounting
of capital accumulation in the ledgers,
the numbers that tally success and failure.

Yet, now, the winners have no future.
The winters have no future.

Yes, we thought to come clear through
country rainbows out of the blue,
cloud shadows on high creek beds,
piles of pillows to arrest the head
but we only burned, slagged Saturday skin,
turning windfalls into the wind.

*

The racket raised by history in our century crosses a locomotive and the revolving barrels of Hotchkiss guns used at Wounded Knee with machine-thudding industrial design. Then there is the slight clink of a blue-flowered coffee cup when Custer's widow turns and looks out the dining car window.

The railroad sealed the doom of American tribal people along with Indigenous Siberians. The shamaness along the Amur River in east Asia said she spoke to the river and listened to what the river said. I don't think colonizing people ever believed you could converse with water. There's no dialogue when long red trickles spill from and pool around bodies in the snow. It is the relentless monologue of the master's narrative. Repetitive guns.

*

The papertrail in Western America was the "Indian" agency stores' ledgers thrown out back as trash once the pages were filled. Picked-up by Natives who drew across the numbers with colors in a palimpsest of perspectiveless scenes recorded by Indigenous eyes, the drawings covered the black and white accounting. The visual world was infinitely greater than the tallied world. One such art-book was actually taken from the waist sash of the corpse of a Northern Cheyenne involved in a skirmish with the U.S. Cavalry. Unlike the fabled Bible in the pocket of the infantryman's shirt that stopped a bullet and saved a life on various Christian war fronts, this bullet went clear through the covers and the pages and into the body, so that blood stained the spine.

As a book dealer or auctioneer of art and artifacts might have said, it left the volume in poor condition.

Not to mention the victim's body.
You could hardly hear the cries of those who were dying
because of the volume of fire.
You could hardly describe the feeling of opening
the archival box in the hushed library
and confronting this book. It could make you scream.
It is the new, wordless, national anthem,
"Oh, say, can you see?"

*

Across the road from a burned-out reservation motel,
faded wooden markers tilt in shifting mounds of sand
that shape themselves to the bodies lying below
wrapped in shrouds— the mounds
burrowed by small animals
amid tipped-over vases of plastic flowers
and tiny, ragged American flags on sticks.

Wovoka was once said to have raised a woman from the dead,
but no one raises him here, buried beside his wife Mary,
where a tumbleweed half-hides his white name, Jack Wilson,
wedged against the worn wood
near the winding of the water and the willows.

Countries

A Silver Gelatin Photograph of Grand Central Station

Beams of light strike the silver clock upon the information kiosk. Consider the long, long wall of ticket windows- each one of which is lit with its destinations north and south and west. You cannot ride a train very far east from Manhattan. But a train from across the Atlantic is due momently, bearing a ghostly passenger list writ on a magic slate that the wind keeps lifting up to erase the manifest. The music that is playing in 1934 in Grand Central Station must be the clop-clop-clop of the hooves of the donkeys in a movement of Ferde Grofe's pop-classic *Grand Canyon Suite*. And in the purse of a woman below, whose hair momentarily shines in one of those falling beams of light, there is a copy of *La condition humane*, one of the novels from that age worth mentioning, and a title that seems prophetic in retrospect- at least when it is translated into English as *Man's Fate* by Haakon Chevalier of Berkeley- whose close friend is the physicist J. Robert Oppenheimer. But this will be later, before Los Alamos, before the Spanish Civil War, but not before the ascendency in Germany of someone who is already digging beneath the feet of millions. Of those below on the floor of this terminal in the winter of 1934, who would believe what the next ten years will bring? They are deep in the depression. Choices are narrowing. Perhaps they cannot even imagine a future as bad as the one many are already enduring. But look- they are still alive, no matter what history may bring, and many must live dynamically- you can see it in their stride. Wouldn't we like to stop the world and keep this still? Wouldn't we ever, knowing what we know now.

Knowing what we know now, all these years later, we see the future no better than the figures in the station, those going to their destinations.

What We Say, How We Say It

'Twang' is as American as 'craps' and 'lounge act.'
Lounge singers wink and croupiers sweep tables of dreams.

Rinky-dink, honky-tonk, you win the derby,
get drunk and forget, wear it to bed.

Mama Kali's nothing more than the name of a horse,
a black horse, a bathtub in Paris, *Les Doors*.

We sling slang, fry cooks flipping flapjacks.
Forkball, knuckleball, screwball, junk.

Daisy Duck licks Donald's butt.
Oil drums march in cartoon madness.

Ed draws the Lucky cap,
the one with the rebus: <u>Last Chance Gas.</u>

Garth yells, Mary Lou howls.
Las Vegas means meadows of green felt.

Dunes, runes, and showgirl presidents—
they dance in a line and kick to high heaven.

"The stars put on their glittering belts."

Poets in the Streets

I shared an apartment in the Haight-Ashbury neighborhood, San Francisco in 1967. My room was in the rear of the apartment on the fourth floor. The room had high ceilings and a three-sided bay window that looked out on the crown of a young redwood tree. Beyond the tree, backyards stretched up the hill toward the foggy heights of Mount Parnassus. I was a student who had applied to become a conscientious objector, but I wanted to be a poet, too, so the room often had an air of superficial creativity: papers scattered across the floor as if they had fallen from Rimbaud's own hand, books open to impressive passages I had underlined, sometimes memorized, and, if inclined, recited to any one who came to visit. Such visits were rather short, not because of my recitations, surely, but because there was only one chair in this room where I slept in a sleeping bag directly on the hardwood floor. The lone chair faced a built-in desk that had been originally intended as a lady's vanity in the nineteen-twenties when the apartment had been built. I often wrote my latest poem far into the night before the cloudy mirror that supposedly faced a lovely woman in her make-up chair. Being quite proud of my ascetic life, I awakened every morning to California sunshine through the open windows of my room and looked up into the boughs of the redwood.

*

One night, in a coffee shop on Mission Street, my friend Lawrence Coulter and I happened to walk in and sit at the counter near an exotic-looking couple. The man was a Mexican; he wore cool sandals and had a distinguished look. We both recognized the woman with the long, dark hair because we had fallen in love with her photograph in Fred McDarrah's book of Greenwich Village poems and photos, late 1950s: *The Beat Scene.* Her name was Margaret Randall, and the man was her then-husband Sergio Mondragon. Together they published a bilingual poetry magazine in Mexico City called *El Corno Emplumado* (*The Plumed Horn*). Avant-garde poetry in American English and translations from everyone rebellious across the hemisphere. Many of the New American Poetry anthology poets published there and the best of them did translations of poetry, everything from Jerome Rothenberg's Paul Celan to Paul Blackburn's Octavio Paz and the Troubadour poets-from Gary Snyder's Han Shan to Clayton Eshleman's César Vallejo and especially Randall's own presentation of Latin American women and militants, so-called "Guerrilla Poets," to recall the title of the then-future (1968) Edward Dorn / Gordon Brotherston book of translations of poets Randall either published or recommended to them: she was the clearing-house. I was already being foreshadowed by later events and developments encountering many influential poets and translators. That was what I had gone to San Francisco to do, and I would encounter these figures in many ways in my life ahead.

Larry and I carefully avoided staring at Margaret Randall, but we did try to eavesdrop on their quiet conversation. At one point, she expounded on "the need for national literature." Perhaps she was speaking of Mexico. To say we were impressed by this beautiful, smart, hip poet wasn't even close. We were groupies who were in awe. We did not rush her for an autograph, but we might have.

*

On another occasion, I went to a dance at California Hall. It was a memorial for a Hell's Angel named Chocolate George, who had died in traffic, or it was a benefit to raise defense money for an Angel on trial for resisting arrest during a Digger parade down Haight Street- I forget which. In truth, I did not want to go, but my friends said the best bands would be there. I guess you couldn't say no to the Hell's Angels.

Steve Miller and his blues band with Boz Scaggs singing, Big Brother and the Holding Company with Janis Joplin singing. Destiny's darling had a few years left to run, and she was in peak form that evening. She blew her way through several songs, and then the band put down their instruments, formed a line across the stage with big smiles and, *a cappella,* sang a tongue-in-cheek gospel dirge, lyrics penned by Michael McClure:

> O, Lord, won't you buy me a Mercedes Benz?
> My friends all have Porsches-
> I must make amends.
> Worked hard all my lifetime,
> no help from my friends.
> O, Lord, won't you buy me a Mercedes Benz?

The Angels could hardly be contained by neo-hip gospel; they got drunk on beer and threw each other all over the dance floor. Avoiding these slam-dancers, the flower children moved off to the sides to observe and avoid the destruction. We were up against the wall, when, through the doors of California Hall, a couple came walking forward and out into the middle of the flying Angels. The man rang Tibetan finger cymbals using both hands, and the woman was a dark-haired beauty. The Angels parted like the Red Sea. Gary Snyder and his date sat down in lotus position in the middle of the dance floor and centered the space for tranquility's sake.

The Angels stopped slinging each other, started to behave themselves. The dance continued on a more civilized basis for the rest of the evening.

*

One day, walking the block from my apartment at Cole and Waller Street to Haight Street, I realized I would have to walk past a gaggle of gooshed bikes, Hell's Angel bikes, and I hoped none of those shit-kicking centaurs might emerge from the seedy apartment building across the street- where they might be snorting long white lines of methedrine, getting way too high and ready to wallop a long-haired hippie.

As I came within fifteen yards of those bikes, who do you think comes strolling out of the entrance of that shabby apartment building? One Hell's Angel dressed in a leather jacket with colors, filthy jeans, terrible, steel-toed, engineer stomper boots. He crossed the street. I'd need to pass by just as he arrived.

The trajectory closed. About to throw caution to the wind and sprint past him, I froze. The Angel was the poet Michael McClure. Who looked as proud as Tyrone Power and as wind-swept-handsome as Shelley. Delicate, as well, so the contrast of the man within the biker get-up and the poet himself practically made me gasp aloud. I quelled myself and continued along. To say I was relieved wouldn't begin to say it.

To be stomped by an Angel or to trip on an iambic foot- there's really no choice. He straddled his bike, kick-started it, roared off to the corner, turned right in the direction of Downey Street where he lived. He was one of the few poets who actually lived in the Haight.

*

Poetry brought me to San Francisco and I studied and wrote diligently to become a poet. Oh, mother, in the shadow of Parnassus, in the howl of the Haight, by the end of my stay in San Francisco, I fulfilled hope and published a poem:

You Kissed Us Both

I once laid idols out for you:
weird, relaxed skulls
growing out of castles
of ordinary clothes.

You kissed us both.
The skulls turned
back into pillows
and we fell asleep
in the grass like stones.

Rolling Stone, San Francisco, February, 1971

Archipelago

- for Helen Bodel

Diving off a tourist island in the Aegean,
I found a stray, intact piece of paper,
a page from a paperback.
It lay on the sandy sea-floor,
Diving close enough,
holding my breath to read it,
I ran out of air and rose again,
leaving it behind like a poem in a dream.

Leaving it behind like a poem in a dream
you have written but can't bring back
from the sleep to the light,
you remain in depths
where you have briefly been,
trying to make sense.

Like grasping at a fish—
the slightest flicker,
the empty fist.

*

They say this is the island where Homer died.
He's probably beneath layers of soil, rocky debris,
ages down in earth-leaves left by waves,
syllabic-boned, flesh a book of dust
below a barren cairn, a worn-smooth boulder
that lost its inscription to rain and wind.

Almost impossibly, sifting time's remains,
you try to conjure those who lived here,
who portrayed themselves in fading mosaics,
those who strolled these dusty lanes,
draped in carelessly articulated phrases,
nattering about markets, the price of gold, honey,
and the great uplift of a courtesan's body.
It was a long time ago in a dark age
between the fall of Minoa and the rise of Athens.

A dark age? It was a time of bards
who sailed the Aegean Sea.
Strumming harps, spinning word-wheels,
they portrayed glories gone wrong
— sacrificed daughters and sons—
found conquests inane
given the sorrow in their wake,
and never underestimated
wrecked rudders, pitched decks
long swell rolls and folderol metrics
in flickering firelight's luminous song.

*

On a Greek bus once, stopped at night,
a roadside in Arcadia,
a blind musician carried his bouzouki case
down the aisle, holding the hand
of a willing samaritan.
Maybe it all happened, as Homer said,
or it was subject to the invented romances
they sing in port taverns, a succession of lovers,
an empress with thoughtful fingers.

I sometimes thought of him, the Bard,
as paradoxical: blind or lost, as we all really are,
but perceptive, especially about the storms,
especially about the sea. I caught him again,
ducking out of the rain into a taverna on Ios
where he danced with a fisherman
from Naxos, holding a handkerchief
gently between them, a stately link
between those hook-scarred hands,
faces tanned, deeply creased.

The painter named Peter hooted approval
drunkenly from the bar, and the
dancers whooped together.

At dusk on the edge of the port,
clouds reflected sunset
the sea glowed red,
wine was invoked
and the lion fed.

*

Nights when the meltemi roared
or during a passing squall's rain,

I listened on the radio
to the Egyptian woman,

to Umm Kolthoum
singing in Arabic

on stations that played
the music of the Middle East—

the desert music that arrives
on waves in the night,

shifting dunes, swooping
troughs rising to peaks,

the life so short,
the craft so small

in the surrounding sea.

*

In an office on Syntagma Square
the old Greek slid his scarab ring
with a screech across the glass-topped desk,
a marker for a direct voyage through the Cyclades
that might lead back, beyond the diaspora,
to a youth in Alexandria, to a library of learning,
to accumulated reason,
to Eratosthenes-like toleration
among warring religions, to benign science and...

Forget it. There was merely a map,
the Mediterranean under the glass-topped desk,
with a hopelessly cheerful cherub
in the empty reaches beyond Crete.

Eternally puffing rosy cheeks,
the cheerful angel portended favorable winds
for a sketched ship on an imagined sea,
not even an inkling of the constant corrections,
the fine keen it takes to reckon the direction
by current, by stars, by a long and constantly
unwavering attention at the helm.

The map's Aegean was a light green
that nearly blended, almost subsumed
the turquoise in the silver Navajo bracelet
my first wife wore,
her wrist delicate beyond landfall
in the real world, on the wide waters
where winds shift quickly,
and no course stays true.

*

Iris is a rainbow. Iris is a girl. Iris is a woman
who thrills.
Iris is a flower, blue and pale blue,
tinged with white, fragile light.
Her scent; violets and rose water.
Her smile envisions
waves, beams, subtle notes, and cool remoteness.
Iris is a color— water floating in oil,
a coil that unravels, a traveler's tale.

Iris empties the trash, sweeps the floors,
stands behind a register and says:

"Yes, M'am, No, M'am,
I'm sorry, Sir, will that be all?"

Iris gets off work, starts home,
but finds herself on an epic adventure,
a long journey into the lives of those
who can never look back.
They scribble messages for her to carry,
songs she must remember,
tales that reveal further tales,
old myths many times twisted
to make them whole, wholly unreal, unreliable.
The heroes spawn confusion and doubt.
They are not really heroes, just lost souls
on a long journey home.
It is the war they leave behind,
but it lies forever ahead
to be remembered, dreamed, a nightmare's omen
she understands. But regrets.

"I have to accept," Iris says. "I ride the wind,
express each syllable in every message sent.
Like a bell from far away, the sound
pleasures the ear— an invisible vibration
of the infinite— ineffable as it disappears."

     *
In a small, glass case on a pedestal

in an early room— a vast national museum—
a Cycladic island sculpture's marble harp
rests on a marble chair arm
and a Brancusi-style bard who's sitting
leans back a marble head to fully sing,
supposedly strumming invisible strings.

A few inches high, starkly white,
the figure's perfect for the early
20th century's rediscovery—
the elegant lines of prehistory.

Once, nimble fingers plucked,
bent notes and streamed music,

mended nets to trace star patterns
in the dark void of distant matter,
disappearing even as we speak,
and helped guide the ships
to thread lives together.
with anchor lines, mooring lines,
the ropes to secure the sails.

Sail away! It was an interconnected web
that spread their lore, their myths,
their lust for far horizons, voyages
to the next and the next island.
It was almost rapturous
and sounded profound depths,
a paradiddle dance
along death's shifty ledges.

> A chorus might sing in rhyme
> about the gods they thought-up,
> treasure they hoped to plunder,
> or how much they loved
> the freedom of dolphins
> following in their wake, breaking
> the sea into foam, breaking
> off, swimming away.

Navigate? Ask those beyond rocking bows
because they roll to meridians unknown
even to sooth song's reckoning.

But who speaks old Aegean now,
steps the dance rhythms anymore,

or sings in a chorus
that might have consoled them?

*

A caretaker at a villa on an island
makes-do with a kerosene lantern,
the wick casting shadows

through gold-lit rooms.
To go out through the courtyard,
back and forth to the doors
he has to cup his palm around
the glass chimney mouth
to guard the flame from guttering out,

while the bell on a lead-goat
rings to the star-herd above the valley,
or the night wind
might leave him in the dark
between the mountains and the sea.

Love's Prognosis

A high-running wave rolls in across sand.
Sitters at cafe tables raise their legs,
scream and shout as the foam
swirls around wobbly chairs.

One waiter watches and laughs, the rest hardly bother to notice.
They stand under the edge of shade,
looking up at the washing machine of imagery and dreams,
the TV under the palm-thatch roof of the Mexican beach bar.

I'm reading Emilio Pacheco doing Catullus in superb *Castellano*.
Catullus was such a kept dog,
hot on the heels of the lady leading him.
Or so he would have us believe in his self-effacing strategy.

But poets have always been hounds
on streets ending in the sea,
hopeless dolts in love with richly deserved desertions,
aching to remain the object of affection,
subject to all the whims as she waves,

waives her attentions and turns to some new Caesar,
who dominates her attention with gifts,
who promises her all sorts of favors,
who savors her slippery-smooth body
as she savors all that is his.

*

She used to come home with that look in her eye.
I was blind, thought we were just fine.
I couldn't see. My problem was literal:
I thought we were married.
Now I believe in checking the car radio buttons.

Her secret boyfriend had his own taste.
I would turn on the car radio, push a familiar button
and what might have been some art in listening
turned into raucous squawk.

Like comedy with a broken heart,
I wasn't laughing— he had
shifted the buttons,
tried it out in different positions.

The radio is a wonder.
You can hear the different dialects:
the preacher, the teacher, the host, the hipster,
the troubled who call in to ask what's wrong with them
And the equally troubled— who think they can answer.

There's the music, too, the soap jingles
in the same washing machine with the blues.
Then's there's the news.
And the news can be cruel.

*

Handsome man, beautiful woman
and all combinations thereof—
deep within, deeper yet
in the shell's turning maze,
I hear the great sea breaking
each of us down to the core,
syllables awash, syllables afloat
on the intake and the outgo.
the breath, the blood's flow,
flooding and ebbing
— sistole/ diastole—
diaspora of surging lust,
forever fleeting love.

*

Yes, Catullus, love is poetry,
and poetry's a crime.

It stole my heart.
stole my honey.

I should have been
up in arms,

but I was adrift
in a contemplative mood.

The Woman in Question

The woman in question asks the man without answers to follow. As soon as the lights go down, they jump out of their seats, duck around the corner of a theater and take a stairway down. They pass through the cutting room and traverse a damp and shadowy region where poets go to sleep on poets' graves. Circumambulating a cloud dome, she leads him on a path where well-dressed people walk dots across Grande Jatte. Entering another realm where sunny flowers grow by way of a ladder, the woman and the man look ahead to a bridge where 19th century locomotives blow steam that rises through the concrete of amusement parks and lifts skirts with a hiss in 1936.

"Iron-age spear fencing creates quite a decorous little square," she says.

"I can agree with that," he replies.

"See how a large ladder dropped in a rain puddle becomes an icon."

"Yes," he smiles, "you're right about that, too." Yet he remains puzzled by the word RAILOWSKY.

A nearby shoe is out of tune, but it summons herders down from the hills so songwriters can finish the last two lines.

"As to why the skulls of Peking Man were first discovered and then later disappeared— I cannot tell you," she says.

"It is a century of discoveries and disappearances, isn't it?"

"Finds and extinctions, yes."

Taking the man down to the river, she points out the opposite shore where a band of irregulars are fighting a uniformed company. The woman says that this goes on forever because each time one group triumphs, they change clothes and sides and keep on fighting.

"Sides of the river?"

"NO— sides of the explanation. For instance, if you wish to terminate leftists, you call them narcotic traffickers."

"What if you wish to exterminate rightists?"

"You only exterminate rightists on rare and special occasions. The opera sets alone are prohibitively costly."

"That is inconsistent."

"Isn't it ever? But why not nether, neither, and nor?

Now they have come to a wall, and the woman calls a halt.

She take out the cock she has brought and kills it, with his help.

They toss the dead cock up and over the wall.

Once the cock is on the other side, it crows.

"I wouldn't have believed it if I hadn't heard it with my own ears," he says.

"Maybe next time you'll believe me when I tell you," she replies.

Lost Chalkline

In spring and summer, in early autumn, too,
ancient Chinese poets wrote poems on pieces of paper,
folded the paper into small boats,
floated the poems down to the next poet
along grassy-banked meandering streams.
Besides the flow of wine to accompany these efforts of navigation,
there must have been an equal delight- grasping the small craft
running past in the current, unfolding the boat to reveal the surprise:

> The sun goes behind the western hills.
> The Yellow River flows to the Yellow Sea.
> Golden Mountain erodes, Middle Kingdom withers-
> This land will be bare rock, thin crows
> By the time I set this poem free.

*

The light switch does not respond. The blackboard's as vague as my plan. The students do not notice yet. They are intent, wiping off desks with thin newspaper pages full of incomprehensible print.

Looming thick, the dust seeps in through broken panes, driven by the wind we walked through, against. It howls out in the dim court-yard full of fine, golden dust from the northwest, the dust that coats the window sills and the raised platform, a stage where Chinese lecturers stand, and the dust tints, I can taste, my teacup rim: *oolong loess*.

"The power is down again," one student says, reading my expres-sion.

"It happens much time," another adds, anxious to try his En-glish, "but you will get used by it."

An unconscious prophet. I must soon mention the perilous preposition, but, at the moment, first day doubts rise in me. Can I even teach? Do not speak too fast! What if they laugh? What if no one un-derstands?

Having all the confidence of a kid chosen last to play right field on a team without mitts, I pick up the chalk and begin to draw the sensual curve, the Gulf of Mexico along Texas and Louisiana shores, down and around obscenely dangling Florida; north past invisible Carolina barrier islands, where isolate communities still speak a Virginia Dare dialect of English I could hardly understand- much less these Han, Hakka, Manchu and Mongolian students.

My map simplifies the indentations and ignores all Atlantic Coast complications, Chesapeake Bay, New Jersey, New York City, on my way to New England, to Hester Prynne, Thanksgiving, and the wake of the Pequod caught in an intricately carved scrimshaw. Making a mess of Maine before I turn west, I blunder my way through the Great Lakes, dying to reach that neatly surveyed line between Canada and the United States which I finally have. It goes well because it can't go bad, until I arrive at the stretch where Montana needs a roof and Alberta requires a floor.

The border disappears into thin American air.

There's no there there, as Gertrude Stein said.

The blackboard's slate has been worn away by all the characters displayed, by all the chalk-dust professors who came before me, and the thousands and thousands of Chinese students who sat there.

I stop, put down the chalk, turn back to the class. How bright and expectant they are! They're ready to learn about American literature. They're prepared for the class to begin, but I am not yet beyond the absence of light, the dust, the erosion and the lost chalkline: the harsh realities of China, 1986.

Before I even begin, I'll need help from these students to understand.

*

In spring and summer, in early autumn, too,
ancient Chinese poets wrote poems on pieces of paper,
folded the paper into small boats, floated the poems
down to the next poet along grassy-banked, meandering streams.

The stream could be read as time,
the unfolding could be read as scholarship,
the delight could be read as delight,
and the wine was wine, after all.

Paul Dresman

But about the slice of moon,
the way night arrives out of nowhere,
and how poets grow cold and weary of the craft
they set forth and collect- I hope to say nothing.

Momentary Poems from China

The lever on the vending machine
has been polished smooth
as the head and belly
of a wooden Buddha.
A man in a Mao cap
sits behind the wheel
of an electronic game,
steering an imaginary car
through an imaginary city.

*

The Return of the
Stock Market to Shanghai

I can't stay away from you
I can't help
but be amused
It's the way
you have about you,
not the things you do,
but that, too,
I can't stay away from you

*

"You understand the intentions
of Protestant missionaries,
don't you?"
Borodin asked the reporter.
"Then you understand mine."

*

The Chinese newspaper says
the majority of Americans
believe in hell. I wouldn't
put it past them.

*

Tao T'ieh

In the museum of Shang pottery,
    your eyes in the glass
        become mine.

*

Swimming down a swift canal
between high stone walls
at the Summer Palace
lost in winter crowds
south of Tiananmen,
dreaming about it.

*

Cerulean blue tiles on
the round house-
not one cloud, not one pilgrim
on the elevated road
to the Temple of Haven.

*

    Bronze Song

At nightfall, the huge log,
pulled back in its cradle
of thick rope,
swings forward through silence
in the Great Bell Temple.

*

A woman, struggling
to carry loaded
buckets on a yoke,
shifts it
to bear the weight
and creates a character
moving through space

Da 大 'Big'

In her human life resigned
to the hardship countryside,
this written symbol,
by its outlines,
wobbles as she goes
down the dusty
indecipherable road.

*

Our two-year-old
said to his big brother
after I read yet another story
featuring Monkey &
The Journey to the West:

"Once, long ago, Buddha
　　touched your hand,
　　　　and you got a shadow-scratch."

*

On the mountains in
the interior- snow
falls all night
while we sleep
and dream
on the mountains
in the interior.

*

Sudden spring storm
bangs open the window above my desk
and the pages of a book flip past
whole chapters of their own accord.
A slight believer in bibliomancy,
I read far ahead of where I am
in Waley's biography of Yuan Mei,

103

18th century Chinese poet
and rake:

"All in all, what's it like
to be aging?"
"A last patch of spring snow,
fingers that won't close
to hold a dripping candle,
a stroke that won't flow
though the brush feels heavy. "

*

Hot May rains falling past
hotel windows
in torpid Taiyuan;
stacked bamboo steamers
full of limp dumplings.

*

You enter a temple on a whim
and, in the dim recess
behind the altar,
grown thin with age,
a hanging silk banner sways.
Bare outlines tracing
once-bright colors,
a lone monk appears
to be wandering
faded mountains and waters.

No matter how long you look,
no matter how long you stay,
the question remains:
Is it rain that falls upon his sleeves
or only the threads below
this world
slowly being worn away?

- Beijing, 1986-87

Purposes to the Western Mountains

Persimmons start to fall in early October.
By November, the golden globes
disappear from their trees
to ripen on farm house window sills,
sometimes dried and sugared,
sent west to Xinjiang and Tibet.

The Chinese treat the Tibetans
like the Americans treat the Cubans—
one of many warped proportions
in this primitive world.

A grinding wheel spins sparks from a dull file.
Yet, we insist that the buckets of dirty water,
the ones we carry everywhere,
do not amount to any hindrance.

Light can be sensed, even in a stone.
Yes, you may be right.
Your civilization may even survive
compressed in a paperweight, a bookend.
Then there is the wind,
and it tears the edges from everything.

They are burning computers
all day in the towers
to extract a little gold.

Put down the ink brush, clear the mirror,
a blank face will be no surprise
the way it looms silently,
the way it hides

the snow of language
falling through the night.

The Returning Student's Story*

Two years in exile from friends and family,
two years from my home in the capital, Beijing,
I can't push open the door of this yurt in Mongolia
because the sheep I herd crowd up for warmth
and the snow hasn't stopped falling all night.

If I tried to call out, no one could hear me.
It's a long way between souls in these grasslands.
I talked twice to somebody else the last month.
I write letters but they're just words on paper,
wishes to the wind on these winter plains.

I miss most a familiar voice that remembers my name.
Maybe someone somewhere will think of me today
because today is my birthday, so I believe,
trying to count back through dark winter nights,
unable to imagine how much time lies ahead.

I want to cry out, but there's nobody remotely near,
so I give up, stoke the stove with more dung.
I live here in the hinterlands on a far frontier
because the Red Guards, in all their wisdom,
thought I was too smart and needed rectification.
I'd like to hear their solution to opening this door.

---

* This poem derived from a prose recollection in a student essay in my wife's ESL class a
Beijing Teachers' University. The student was part of a group of men and women returning
to finish their education in 1986, interrupted by the Cultural Revolution twenty years before.

Kai-yu Hsü Knocks on Zheng Min's Door

When Hsü comes to visit, you refuse to remember him,
old classmate, old friend long gone to America
where he translated your poems
and then returned to China to write a book
about a history of contemporary literature
more bitter than he could have guessed.

Post-Nixon, the Party glad-hands him.
You offer a cold shoulder—
no recognition, can't remember him, you say,
shaking your head
even as he looks beyond you,
over your shoulder in the doorway,
the flat inside the Qinghua compound.

He recognizes taste in the furnishings,
in the Western classical music playing
on a phonograph, sees you again—
the young woman in braids,
Cheng Min in Wade-Giles,
who sang beautifully, alone
among the graves
at the wartime campus in Kunming,
a fellow student who practiced
a fierce independence
by refusing to sit at a desk
while the difficult philosopher— Feng Yo-lan— lectured,
preferring to stand outside the open windows instead,
distancing herself and defending poetry.
("I've always been lonely," she told me.)

All the while, his minder looks on, as does
the neighbor-snoop across the corridor at her door.
It is the Cultural Revolution, and foreigners are suspect,
especially educated Overseas Chinese.
Your refusal to remember him
led him to ponder what was meant.
Some of this he sensed:
the extent he couldn't guess.

107

Leaving your apartment building that day,
he said in his book
that his bicycle hit a rock,
that he dropped or lost his pen.

Your silence left him little to say.

             *

Kalli means 'good,' and good has been written—
it is calli-graphy, 'beautiful writing'
in the Greek, comes from

                    the Sanskrit,
        kalya,
                    'healthy.'

Beauty presupposes health,
not just black ink on white snow
long after the language goes.

Books were palm leaves
bound together, *book*
means to be bound, could even be
leaps always going outward,
crossing continents, leapfrogging
lotus petals on a calm pond.

That the cosmos is reflected in thought
and life rotates accordingly—
sometimes chaotically, sometimes disastrously,
sometimes with all the parts in harmony.
You need a pen and ink and character,
not just characters, but character.
The old poets showed me.

             *

"Oh, I treated him so badly when he came to visit me in China."
    Because I knew exactly what she meant- her puzzling behavior
in his account of the meeting- I played dumb in the hope that she might
go on to explain herself.

"Oh, you did?" I said.

"Yes, he came to see me, and I pretended not to remember him. What could I do? It would have been bad for me, for my family, and for him."

She was probably right. There we were, walking in southern California sunshine with all the beautiful students of worldly success in their robust health and fashionable styles, and there we also were, talking about a moment of nuance and avoidance one day years before halfway across the world, in a China that very few of the passing students between classes would ever hear about or begin to understand. They had innocent smiles that played across their faces; faces I know well, being a Californian, too, and then there was Min, tears verging in the shine of her eyes, in the midst of the bouncy, collegial atmosphere. Hardly anything in the lives of those around us provided the experience or the insight to understand such confusion over identity and belief. A North American's reasons for paranoia might amount to child's play compared to the machinations, denunciations, punishments and executions in the chaos of twentieth century China- especially during the Cultural Revolution when suspicion and violent recrimination were the order of the day.

Kai-yu Hsü was a bright scholar, professor, poet, translator and literary and political commentator, but he had been in California too long. He had pushed himself naively into Min's life, asked leading questions, ignored the possible consequences. As she told me, not only his minder accompanied him, but, when she had opened her door, the neighborhood snoop, who lived directly across from Min, stood at an open door to observe and listen to what was going on. When my wife Christine and I went to Beijing to teach, when we approached Min's door for the first time, the same neighbor opened her door to observe us. Poignantly, Min could not make any apology to Kai-yu because, a few years before she arrived, after several days of drenching rain, the hillside above his residence had been inundated, and he was killed in a mud slide on his Marin County home. Ignoring warnings, he had rushed into the house to retrieve manuscripts, a true poet and scholar to the last.

Yet, Hsü at least knew that something was amiss on his visit to Zheng, and what he claimed about her loneliness remains true.

When we toured northern California together as she read her poetry in Chinese at several venues and I provided the English versions, she mentioned her loneliness to me. Due to the death of her young parents, she had gone to live with relations at a mine in Hunan province. They performed their filial duty by raising her, but they showed very little affection and interest in her. Given that the mine's location was isolated, Zheng Min grew up lonely in China. In part, this accounted for her deep interest in music. Every week, she told me, she had looked forward to the Firestone Hour on a shortwave radio, the American program that played classical Western music. The music had a deeply emotional connection for her.

As she spoke, we were in my car, driving south from San Francisco on our way to a community center in San Jose where she would be reading her poetry. The freeway led through the hills of the California coast range, and, when she had related her story about her loneliness and the music that comforted her, I asked, "Min? Would you sing for me?"

She became embarrassed. "Oh, I don't sing any more!"

But I persisted, and she assented.

She sang the lyrics of a traditional poem from the T'ang dynasty that had been set to music.

As she began to sing (and I glanced over from watching the freeway ahead), an aura appeared around her- as it happens sometimes when poets or singers perform. Her voice was no longer the voice of an older woman. Instead, her voice was the voice of a young girl, and it transformed her. She sang very well, and the passing landscape, the cars and the freeway- they dropped away and disappeared into the song she sang because she felt the song in the depths where a song abides and rises on the breath, inspiring the singer and whoever hears it. Even in another language, another tongue, the singer's conviction rings clear. Then I looked straight ahead and saw the cars blur, straight ahead because I didn't want her to see my tears.

*

Once, in his classroom at San Francisco State
in the sic transit *Gloria Mundi* year of 1968,
Professor Hsü suddenly stopped discussing
the lines of a Chinese poem about a farewell,
paused, looked up at the class where we all sat,

and told us about the last time he paused
at the spirit wall and saw his aged father

across the compound courtyard,
the last time he said goodbye, Sichuan, 1945.

Pass your hand across your eyes.

Now Hsü stands behind a pillar
and curls of white paper stream from his hair.
The blind fortune teller taps a snakeskin fish drum.
Dressed in sack cloth and white caps,
a courtege should be following,
scattering dead money along a Chinese hu-tong,
but Hsü's life closed in California,
and who can say which was his home?
His own teacher, Wen-I-do, once wrote:
      "Let me not deceive you. I'm no poet
      even though I love the integrity of white gems,
      the blue pines and the immense ocean.
      The sunset on crows' backs
      and the dusk woven with the wings of bats..."

The Uses of Poetry[*]

"Coming back to China, I rode in the bed of an open truck with a dozen Tibetan pilgrims returning from Lhasa to Chamdo. Normally, it's a three-day trip, but it took us ten. The truck kept breaking down, and we ran out of food. So we bought a yak and cut it up. I prefer parts of the yak raw. Some parts are better than other parts, and you can't cook yak in the back of a truck. The roads were bad. The truck would chug up a hundred switchbacks in low gear to the next pass and come down a hundred switchbacks on the other side in low gear to climb up the road to the next pass. We got bounced around. Then we would break down. The drivers would figure out a way to fix it while we all sat on the side of the road and looked out over distant ridges. Then we'd climb back up on the bed and get bounced around again.

"In the middle of nowhere, we blew part of a head gasket. There was no spare. There was no parts store, not on the road to Chamdo. So I volunteered the cover of my paperback anthology of American poetry. A Khampa cut it to shape with one of those scary knives they carry it at their waist. It fit the head and off we went again, up and down across Tibet.

"The entire distance, the Tibetan pilgrims had been chanting *Om Mani Padme Hum*. It's their main mantra: the *jewel in the lotus*. I had gone along, chanting with them. After awhile, you don't even think about it. We were going over another pass, thirteen thousand feet high. This time there was black ice. The truck started to slide sideways. There was a cliff. All the Tibetans sped up their chant, and I switched to The Lord's Prayer. I was into the first part, "Our father who art..." That's when the driver must have turned the wheels into the slide, threw it into reverse with a terrible transmission grind, pulled the emergency brake, I don't know. He got the tires to grip on the gravel shoulder. We stopped just at the edge. The truck was rocking, the engine had died, and we all stood up in the bed, looking down into the abyss."

---

[*] This account was told to me by an American named Jay who went by the Chinese name "Ding," a mountain-climber and graduate student in physics at Beijing University (Beida) who lived in a Chinese dorm— six to a room, a pair of three-tier bunk beds in a space about as wide as this page. He was also a guitarist in the first rock band in the capital: The Beijing Underground.

School Business

Perhaps it wasn't the best idea about teaching that I have had, but now that we're all here, somewhere beyond the Western Hills outside Beijing, I'm glad I decided to have the students go on a term-end picnic. We must be somewhere near the Dragon Pool and Wild Mulberry Temple because it's the same stream. But we're downstream somewhere.

Chen explained it. I couldn't really follow his finger across the map and study the written characters at the same time. The bus driver nodded when I asked. What did that mean?

But now we're here by the stream, and most of the students are having a good time. Some haven't stopped running along the banks since we arrived. Others have spread newspaper pages at the water's edge, sat down protected from the mud and dipped their bare feet in the water. A couple of the young men, pant legs rolled up, stand in the shallows. The water's cold enough, even in this bright sun, to make them fold their arms and shiver.

It's a pleasure to be outside in afternoon light, out of the city. I can get lost in the babbling current over rocks, and I nearly forgot! I must collect their term projects. If I don't do it now, I know I won't remember to do it later.

Moving among the students, they reach into their bags and hand me their papers. I'm surprised that they all have used soft, bright-colored folders I haven't seen in China- maybe because these are the term projects, and this is the semester's end. Everyone has given me their work- except for her.

She's the young woman who sits in the back of the class and smirks. She's also the only woman brave enough to wear a bathing suit today, and she lets the straps fall, as she struts in front of all of us- displaying herself. She is beautiful, it is true, but formidable. I've never had the sense she believes in any of this school business.
I must ask her for her project.
"It's in your briefcase already," she says.
I look into my briefcase and something is there.

What a strange woman! It is a book in a wooden frame. But when I pull it out of the briefcase, there is nothing between the frame, no pages. You can look right down through where the book should be, down to the stream or up to the sky.

"That is the Book of Blue," she explains.

I'm confused. Unfastening the clasp, I open the hinged frame to see if I have missed something, if something might have been over-looked. Or hidden within.

Bees begin flying out of the open space I have opened, swarms of them. It is amazing and frightening in the dream.

She stands before me laughing as the bees fly up between us to the sky.

I try to close the frame, but she grasps my hand. She is stronger than I am.

"No," she says, "before you close it, tell me: What will the grade be?"

Where Do We Go From Here?

Hawaiian ghosts were thought
to go to sea. Crop circles
supposedly appear
in the wake of alien visitors
who voyage from distant stars
just to fuck with our heads.
Listening to new music,
you finally catch on.
Many murders are covered-up
by imprisoned souls
quoting scripture. That
passed so fast, you think
you imagined it.
Sheltered from the storm,
sea turtles raise their heads
landward,
driven over the reef
and into the lagoon.

The pianist was born in Tashkent.
His mother met Anna Ahkmatova
eating oranges and drinking vodka.
Fifty-thousand nomads
climbed over the snowy mountains
to reach the grasslands and survive.
Later they were purged
as part of a rectification
to return the revolution
to its truest principles.

The pioneers found pots and pans
others before them left behind
on the Oregon Trail
and fashioned shoes for the oxen
to walk across the blazing plains.
Kaya is a Tartar born in Ankara
who now lives in Haleiwa
on the north shore of Oahu.
Russian ghosts are everywhere,

the things they leave behind.
The empty shell of the turtle
straddled the beach at high tide.
I imagine I came from central Asia
like everybody else in Europe
once upon a time. Nomadic life
suits those with get-up-and-go.
Wearing skins can be lousy,
but Appaloosa underpants
might really excite someone.

The market falls
another five-hundred points.
I think I'll have a potato.

"Every freeloader on the north shore's
here for half-price salad night."
A sudden downpour
scatters the diners
on the terrace.
They all rush in
holding plates.
Sometimes it is not our fault
that slips, but our neighbor's
continental shelf,
and that's why the boats
get tossed around,
end-up on the docks.

The Milky Way sprays stars
in a wide band across the sky.
The entire capitalist system
appears to be reinvigorated.
A terrible beauty is borne
on the backs of underlings.
All things come due:
wet bare feet, thirteen-inch
centipedes, a man in the dark
dancing for all he's worth.
Paddling out,

the waves jumped up,
breaking further
on distant reefs, and the crack
and roar got loud. I
wondered how I was ever
going to get back in
because the reef pass,
a narrow channel,
was running too fast
to paddle against, so
I had to ride a wall of foam
over the reef, and it tore off
my fins, and there were too many
coral heads to paddle around,
so I had to get off and swim,
sometimes sideways
across the lagoon, dragging
the board behind
on a leash.

The schools of bright-colored
tropical fish scattered
before me, and
I nearly ran into a needle fish
standing perfectly still
straight up and down.
I could look clear
through it, so I didn't even
see it, until it
dipped away from my face.
Was it ever even there
where I couldn't see it?
This is not an advertisement
for God, because a needle fish
in real life is far more
impressive in its absence
than anything you imagine.
Imagine this: we all once swam
in the same sea together,
and we will again.

The River Remembers

- for Tom Marshall

Surely, a coincidence—
the smoke alarm goes off as
proselytizers ring the doorbell.

*

Diamond Matches!
The Laughing Buddha
strikes anywhere.

*

The moon by day chases memories,
pale imitation of the moon at night,
strange reflection of the moon inside.

*

She recalled crude So Cal drive-ins
with a couple of palms, the boys
polishing their dashes, quick and gone.

*

Love's passing boat— a small sail
across a vast wall of windows
in a mansion yet to be built.

*

The floor falls away due to a fault,
product of plate raised against plate,
the mouths to feed, the acreage.

*

Red-shoulder hawk, backyard tree-tops,
when I turn away, she likes to play,
flying low to skim my scalp.

*

Locked-down, they finally made face-time,
the hungry wolf who'd like to be friends
and *la belle dame sans merci.*

*

Assumptions can be assumptions,
bliss can be bliss—
even the sliced lemon says yes.

*

Weldon's last wrench—
clinging to life, leaping
from the Golden Gate Bridge.

*

Look deep enough in water,
you'll discover far off
the faint outline of a fin.

*

The surfer wouldn't go out that day: too big.
"Besides," he said, "if I drowned in Mexico,
my wife would never forgive me."

*

Evening snow at Willamette Pass,
dead battery down in the valley,
the skis go back in the garden shed.

*

November moon on icy ridgepoles,
I'm already old. Leaves glide past,
wild geese flee to the south.

*

The river passes us by.
We can't step into
the same river ever!

*

Nearing the sea,
dreaming of springs,
the river remembers everything.

Naming

Out the window, above a brook, April blossoms,
orange trees, lemon trees, irises purpling dawn and dusk,
granite boulders, my sentimentalities, a red wheelbarrow
full of blue leaves, cypresses on the ridge,
snowy peaks on the Sierra Nevada in the distance—
what can I convey about perspective? This isn't California.

*

In a Mission-style, security-gated community for senior citizens in southern California, a developer exercised his poetic license by assigning the street names to Spanish poets and composers. It made a certain Hispanic sense. So there was a *Calle Neruda*, a *Calle Alberti,* poets of exile and revolutionary politics, poets that scarcely could call anywhere home. Well-traveled, to be sure: one was from Chile, the other Spain. They led lives that sometimes were more than exciting, and it left them weary.

Pablo Neruda survived to die in Chile, at the time of the American-backed military coup in 1973, while Rafael Alberti was a refugee from the Spanish Civil War who was exiled to Buenos Aires, Argentina, the same city where Neruda had been in 1933 when Federico Garcia Lorca came from Spain with a theatrical troupe and his plays, including Lorca's first success about the early 19th century liberal heroine and eponym Mariana Pineda of Lorca's native Granada.

In 2000, the Chilean poet and publisher Jorge Lagos Nielsen took Jesús and Janine Sepúlveda, Christine Seifert and me to a table on *Avenida Mayo* in Buenos Aires where Neruda and Lorca drank coffee in the grand *Cafe Tortoni-* Lagos pointed out the framed drawing on the wall behind us that Lorca left for the cafe. Lorca wasn't a Communist, but, in 1936, the Fascists in Spain executed him anyway, maybe for being gay, or for poetry, or for his plays, or his *duende*. It was akin to killing Shakespeare. Unforgivable.

The California developers named a street for Lorca too- amid the white stucco houses with red-tile roofs in southern California. Lorca and Cervantes and Rodrigo wind around through the lawns and palms, and the weather's similar- if nothing else pertains.

*

The guide in Manuel de Falla's house
shows us the bullet holes of 1936,
the one through an interior door,
two through a nearby wall,
and one more that must have shattered his soul.
He shows us the table where the four Spaniards—
poet Lorca, painter Picasso, guitarist Segovia
and our host, the modernist composer,
sat in 1922 during the festival of Cante Jondo: "Deep Song."
It is a small room, a small table,
and the chairs seem small, too.
On the sideboard, a stringless zither—
a gift for de *Falla* from García Lorca. It is quiet
in the house of the composer where nobody dwells
but the relics of a life gone by, long concluded.

There's an anonymous ditch in the countryside
where Lorca's buried.
The plays he might have written have been buried with him,
the players' words entwined with those murdered beside him.
It is a stark tableau for the end of the second act.
The guide thanks us for our donation, and we exit.

The afternoon wind turns dappling leaf shadows
on the road that climbs
up the hill behind us to the Alhambra.
You can hear the restless wind
in the eaves, among the trees and through the narrow,
twisting lanes of Granada.

With a voice from the San Fernando courtyards in Cádiz,
with a howl of gravel and broken glass
and sorrows born in the darkness on the Roma road,
Camarón sang the poems of Lorca's *Romancero Gitano*,
poems that came to Federico from Sacromonte
rhythms and lore
in a life terminated by roped wrists, an impromptu firing squad.

Paul Dresman

A stringless zither is like a white horse on a moonless night,
a mountain covered in snow hidden by clouds,
a ghost who sings a song lost in time.

Entropic Calypso

A truly sincere ghost from a country where palms grow
saw a bird of unknown origin being born from a light bulb.

The new-born shook its fresh wings,
caught a stir of breath on a tropical breeze,

rose from the palm tree, circled
the ghost's head and began to sing.

The bird did sing anything sweet.
The bird did not sing anything pretty.

The bird sang like a rivet under stress
And left a smell of barbiturates on the breath.

The fire bird sang flames and visions,
a discordant song about Prince Charming

while Sleeping Beauty stayed home
and fumed and smoked in bed.

A god named Yawn licked a charred stick,
set a long fuse, and the fire bird flew

faster and faster around the ghost's head, singing

"One particular, two vehicular, three parts read,
four pragmatic, five enigmatic, six parts lead."

Encounter in La Selva

Because my partner got sick, she stays in camp while I go out to climb one of the unexcavated Mayan pyramids. Centuries past, the forest grew up and over them. You can scramble through trunks and branches, hand over hand.

It goes faster than I'd have thought. I stop a few times, breathless, sweating, a little tired, a little scared of meeting a viper, but talk myself into going higher, up and up to the apex.

Under the overgrowth, deep in the understory, leaves brushing my cheek, I suddenly find myself looking into the eyes of a spider monkey, a baby wrapped around her neck.

We're a few feet apart, the length of my arm. The monkey studies me momently, shrugs. I'm nothing special and she goes on purposefully, hand over hand in the limbs. Intent, distant, a spider monkey baby face gazes back at the intruder.

        *

        Humans make much of their own death
        with extravagant monuments,
        rituals and relics, not to mention
        the gods riding in a death canoe
        carved on a bone in a tomb,
        or all those questions
        floundering in religion
        and who's been jettisoned.
        Humans keep monkeys caged in zoos
        and for the purpose of experiment,
        the arguable necessity of testing.
        Caged, weighed, fed to be subjected
        to such trials and tribulations
        you might as well call science a religion, too,
        a brutally sacrificial one at that,
        but we seldom have a chance to meet,
        face to face, our accomplices in the wild,
        bison particles, Bohm conversations,
        where, it turns out, they hardly care

to share our refined sense of wonder.
Yet that astonishes us, enough
to touch our spirit.
      The gods are close
            and ride with us.

The Eye of a Strange God

- for Alexis Figueroa

1

Lowry was thrilled and perplexed by love.
He sped through time, a lighthouse
beam out of focus, a ship adrift at sea.
It was a handheld camera kind of writing.
We can't quite grasp the closeups.
Other faces wobble and warp in the drunkard's gaze.
Gardens race off like a swatch of Monet
seen through the window of a passing train.

2

This volume stands naturally on a rough-cut shelf,
a squatter's shack built out over northern waters,
a dwelling in British Columbia destined to burn.
This volume could appear
in a number of second-hand shops, a radio
behind the counter with swing music for foxtrots,
that quirky, jerky 1920s jazz with guitars and banjos.

In his youth in England,
Lowry played in such a group, flash-famous
on a cover of sheet music, stole someone's song,
played to the pitch and tilt,
a dancer's hand in the small of a back
to tattoo a suggested romance,
a trip to the moon in a silvery spoon.

You can hear the moan behind the characters
who appear on deck. It is a horn in the distance
that the invisible figure in the lighthouse mirrors.
A natural and irresistible aristocrat, the author sabotages
the whole shebang— modernism's dubious inheritance.
Modern man cannot be satisfied,
let it all die... but record the mind's stuttering shimmers
as the light persists within everything witnessed.
The light speaks volumes about loss and drift.

Lowry preferred Faros. They must have reminded him
of his quickly lost youth, young swain in a suit
on a bandstand, playing a ukulele,
looking off into the middle distance above the dancers.
A mirrorball spun in the dimness of space
and dazzled its reflections,
streams of light from a fragmented stream of mind.

3

A short siesta near noon. Boom,
he was back up, drinking.
By the time the sun withdrew, he flew
Through various cantinas around the *mercado*.
A gun fired with regularity up in the hills.
Someone was hunting, it was hoped.
The air filled with cracks, matched
the mirror where he sat at the bar,
looking at himself through the honey of the smoke.

4

The temple stands on an offshore island.
Isolation becomes its own prize,
security surrounded, virginity
or ignorance of dirty, low, dishonest decades.

I inquired about the place, the shack where he squatted.
But today's coastal villagers shook their heads.
A big ferry from Nanaimo churned past,
the waves washed over the rocky point with firs,
a Chinese painting of the Song or Ming.
They said, "An author? Like Harry Potter?"
You may as well dive from a deck railing
to catch the effect of his life after Mexico,
or sun yourself for years in B.C. out at the end of a beam,
a dream of green mountains down to an inland sea
where he put the finishes touches on Under.

It may as well be "Under Popo"
with Penelope and the Weavers,
A famous stream-of-consequence musical, mad
with Modernist momentum, blind Joyce, Finnegan space.

127

5

A flicked wristwatch, dislocated head.
You could take a lighthouse, a Faro, and stand it
on its end, a burning cigarette
on the scarred and chipped table,
get a voice to talking till it runs
with logorrhea and orders tequila.
The *cantina* is a sea, swirling.
The others drink to
finding their way through the fog.
Getting high is high theatre,
the drama we all require, lime and salt,
the sudden sweep of the spotlight
to keep you on the rocks.
So is love, and love among drunks
requires a high tower from which
we may leap together
into the sea, unless we can
climb the winding stairs
with the keeper.
The keeper is the one who remains,
a card in a tarot deck
yet to be invented.
You could perform the same trick.
You could spiral to the top
and blind yourself with the intensity
even a small candle becomes
on the banks of circular mirrors.

6

"He who letteth the rain fall on the just and unjust
and without whom not a sparrow falls to the ground."

Wasn't around, said to be dead, the shack burned,
papers scattered, perfect sonnets in one era
gone out the other, dead in England, drowned.

Malcolm Lowry deserved his death
passed out, drowned in his own vomit.

This was a century that died of drunkenness,
drunk on battleships, drunk on bombers, drunk
on barbed wire, drunk on machine guns, drunk
on dance, drunk on drugs, drunk with purpose,
drunk by design, drunk with power, drunk
and vomiting, drunk and disorderly, dead drunk.

7

A table drifts beneath the waves
and there it is: a beacon
with five drowned men sitting,
the glasses still in their hands,
the cards remaining face down.

"It is, after all, an old film.
They used to show it at the Phoenician
On Grand Street. Or was it Main?
I first went to see it in the old days.
The men still wore their hats. They sat
with their hats in their laps."

The film unwinds in the dreamy dark.

She begins to lift this and reveal that.

You decipher the glyphs— the veins and their forecast.
A poet projects white writing,
a stylized lantern apes a candle.

Its beams sweep across unchartered waters
while dolphins misguide pleasure boats.

A man with swag comes in the picture.

Lighthouse keepers hover in the background, ghosts.

The film is about this city,
as this city was,
all the extras
dead and gone.

A projector's beam unwinds the real

and we fall asleep to the cries of gulls.

After a Line by Blaga

- for Jesús Sepúlveda

"We are guests on the porch of a new light."

Speaking back and forth in our poor second languages,
cracking calm nouns in half, truncating the militant verbs,
throwing around infinitives as it they were infinitely serviceable,
we gesture our way through a conversational marketplace,
extolling watermelons that belong to Lorca and Ginsberg,
Whitman's *bandanas* and Neruda's ten-thousand hats
sailing in the breeze down from the Andes, a Mistral
fluttering the hair of a woman selling flowers in Temuco,
or that other mountain wind that is Incan and obdurate
and oblique in the ears of César Peru's *burro*
on the hungry boulevards of France.

Authorities swoon and die at the Real Academia.
The Oxford English Dictionary spontaneously combusts.
We fracture our languages in a flagrant disregard
in order to capture the poets we keep in mind
on the streets of Santiago or San Francisco. We dislocate
the entire cordillera to run on a jut through Eugene
by way of a small tectonic fault that cuts clean.

Just met, this kind of talk takes us off into Region 19.
We're a little bit wild, a little bit drunk
-it's a Friday night party!- romantic and cruel
and mysteriously American
down the length of these Americas-
prancers of the antipodes who infuse
slender poems into tight *ritmos*
in long, loose, samba-drum lines at carnival time.

We speak on the heels behind luminous tracks
that the silversmithing poets lay down,
and of the soles that are just beyond reach
when bankers bend over to touch the ground
and digits run out of money to count.

Seeds have been broadcast as syllables said
and we lean and sway on the deck
of an earthbound ship, surrounded
with dancers catching their breath
and drunks who laugh to be lifted
and tossed in their heads
like small children in their father's hands.

We are guests on the porch of a new light,
invitados en la baranda del mundo nuevo.

Babylonian Radio

Babylonian Radio

I

The river Eridanus runs along sky's horizon—
light years from the sources.
Homer called it the Ocean Stream,
so too the Babylonians, the Egyptians and many Asians.
It flows through our dreams. Carrying us
into the labyrinth to lay to rest the inner beast,
pursue tranquility, practice an art,
balance the yin with the yang, resist
trembling anxieties with resolute clarity
to spin beneath a windfall of stars.

On a cooling evening in the dark
amid beds of orchestrated flowers,
you may follow vines winding
up, down, around an arbor
to constellate humans and beasts,
draw imagination's lines
through time and space.
The overhead galactic dome wheels
each night's progression of heaven.
Lore embellishes stories, theatrical
comets pass, fiery meteors streak.
The gods come down to earth
to tell the tales, enhance the spells.
There's wonder and poignancy
because, after all, we're mere mortals,
this felt flesh and solid bone
riding through space on a globe.

*

A swan flies from a midnight pond
to be slain by a far-off archer.
The bull's horns are all we need
— a pair of bicycle handlebars—
to rough-out the body of the beast.

He waits at the core of the maze,
the id, for the Athenian to free him.
lest he be released to wreak havoc.
Liberation can arrive like Elijah
with the priests of Baal, a beast.
He felt free to cut four-hundred throats,
for God's sake. By another god's grace,
a corona diadem floats overhead, crown
for a princess abandoned on a beach.
Ariadne went off with Dionysus:
"What a lovely couple they made…"
Her analagous sister Iphigenia
was sacrificed by a warrior father
to calm the waters, sail the war ships
for conquerors who worship war.
By the ruse of a rocking horse,
you win the war, but home is hell.
In a thousand rips, a tapestry splits,
the wife and mother takes revenge.
In a hot bath, a deep soak,
blood runs like mad. "Eridanus,"
Cassandra said, "will flow red."
Agamemnon stiff, Agamemnon numb.

Wars will always come back home.

The mind will be unable to find itself
after the towers are smashed,
the gardens torn and burned,
trees turned into black sticks.
Survivors crippled, stumbling
across Anatolia or back to Iowa City in a jet,
left with a duffel bag on a corner in Murmansk,
drifting to sleep in an L.A. heroin haze.

Riderless, grazing in the June grass—
a saddled horse at Little Big Horn,
Germans in January at Stalingrad,
an old veteran across the street
hissing through missing teeth.

"We started out with twenty tanks
up on the Yalu. We heard the bugles,
then the Chinese came. That was the end
of our unit— all those men.
Just the two of us on the run.
We never slept. Or we couldn't have lived."
Many survivors never sleep right since.
The Cheyenne shaman rode off
from burning boxcars on the tracks
with a bolt of calico tied to his pony's tail.
Unwinding the skein across the Western plains,
it came to include a Numu Paiute medicine man
in the wake of a departing train,
the logger's mind blown away
in a lightning flash. A visionary world
revealed itself in the crown of his hat.

In the Odyssey, a series of trials and perils
describe how you find your way from war to home,
a set of temptations and diversions so intriguing,
you can hardly shield your eyes from their beauty
or from their terrors. In consequence, the ancients
found a way past the monsters at the core of memories
by rites into the initiation of mysteries, an escape
from the hovering fear of hungry beasts
— the dire bears deep in the cave—
the spectre of death who stalks every woman
giving birth and walks beside every man on the hunt,
in the rush and the blood. Every child is born
out of nothing, a quantum of everything.
Time extends when you look into space.
The light in a newborn's eyes, one and the same.
Vulnerable, helpless, we gather together
to defend one another. Stoke the fire,
sing the common song, fall into laughter
to stave off disaster. You have to meet fear
to overcome fear, follow darkness to a reckoning
by telling yourself to stop thrashing against the sea,
by going fearlessly into water that keeps you afloat,
find the way by riding the current,

give yourself over to it, go deep, find release
in the nothing that sustains this unlikely existence,
life's perplexing, confusing, ungainly conundrum—
riding windy fire across the wide heavens.

*

In a cavern, swimming in a stream
running deep underground, the modern explorer
held his breath under rock to reach a further pool
where he arose from the black water
to breathe again— an inner chamber,
the sacred space of the painters and the rites.
It was as if you went out into night's empty expanse,
into the stars that parade a dream's own world,
found yourself dead, to be reborn, visions
out of leaves thrown into fire,
breathing smoke, enduring hunger,
dancing all night out through imagination,
tearing the flesh of sacred mushrooms
to travel far down passages into the earth,
deep in the body, inside the lobes
tracing natural lines along rock crevices
that suggest bison horns, antelope spines,
sloth noses, wag-tail wild dogs. You trace
a running red, or a yellow ocher line,
a meridian of the marvelous,
in the flickering pine-torch light
that suggests the motion of all life,
that oceanic pitch and roll
we might have once known
adrift in amniotic fluency
amid the body's sacred beauties.

There is a winding labyrinth to follow.
Water running eons underground
carves its sinuous way through rock.
Thus, the Tao. It takes a precipitous fall,
a dizzying plunge to dance with the bear,
dance with the lion, ride the backs of horses,
transform into the she-fox and the he-wolf.

howl in the caverns till the lit pine pitch dies,
the flute rising to fall to skin-stretched drums.
Then you must feel your way out.
As in birth, we come from echoes of echoes.
The darkness below ground, the darkness inside.
Where have I been? Where are we going?
"You have no face. You have no name."

*

I'd like to conjure a seer who thrills
with a high, pure poem, a magic dancer
with an animal head, a shadow floating
over a cave wall to sabotage Plato.

It's a contrary map of the cosmos.
a cross-dressed sensuality that tempts us
into dancing all night by firelight,
entwined arms and wrapped legs,
enrapt in the righteousness of rhythm,
in purely ecstatic vivacity
coming once, twice, thrice
to undermine the priestly lie
of the institutionalized. Right!
I'd ramble in the languages swirled
around the foundations of thought—
the graffiti that scrimshaws
the spiralled Tower of Babel,
that ziggaurat of genetic rockets.

Or sit back, relax and get low
in the glow of a Chet Baker solo
on nineteen-fifties West Coast radio
tuned to the stations of the desert.
Babylonian frequencies depend
on a suspension of disbelief.
The hanging gardens of Hammurabi
drape strings of stars to glitter
above the Mojave, only to be displaced
by the hard light of dawn, its long
shadows that project against

the rain-shadowing mountains
and the strange reflective glass
turned hard and shining at Yucca Flats.
The die is cast. The cherries line-up
Le rouge et le noir spin for fortune
on fortune's own disproportionate wheel,
and we go round again into a new day,
a return on eternity. Babylon
is a state of mind, where dancers
tease time, and the desert sun's
a bright thorn by day,
the moon a hidden pear at night
way out west, way out on the edge
where warm rain drifts down
like lace from distant clouds.
Her flowing hair is misted.
Terra turns in radiance
while distant thunder rolls rumble
across the mesas and the hoodoos,
through the canyonlands
in cannonades that set us on edge.
Simon Ortiz in the kiva at Acoma
knew what the ravens said. I know
how they glide close, past your shoulder
as you descend, handhold by foothold,
down the cliff to the water, mesa rock
scraping your delicate cheek—
red ocher streak— a black wing feather
sashsaying and seesawing downwind.

There are those peripheral omens we catch
when we follow a rabbit down the hole
till geometric patterns devour
the ego, leave a self spinning
around in limbo, drowned
in the wash of a sonic wave,
in the wake of a vaporus trail

just as I sense, just as I know
we arrive again

in the world above
out of the world below.

Water runs wind-torn leaves
to spin downstream as the last star fades
in dawn's shivering cold.
A pair of wild swans
silently fly the river, round a bend,
vanish into the mountains. Distances
put the world back together again.

You could hear a flight
forty thousand years ago
if you played this flute
carved from a swan's wing bone.

*

When Moses was a baby
Floating in the reeds,
His mother's woven cradle
Made the Nile fall asleep.

"Fibs," my grandmother said.
"You'll get in trouble telling fibs."

You can't part the seas.
You can't swallow the tablets
brought down from a mountain.
But it is miraculous story, and we love it
when the light shines a path to freedom
and the slaves are released,
the slaves of the Egyptians, the slaves of the Greeks,
the slaves of the American plantations,
slaves of colonialism, industrialism,
slaves delivered from the infernal systems,
wage slaves and received idea slaves,
everyday slaves under control,
slaves of closed circuit cameras,
locked-tight minds, slaves under God
and the bling masters of collection plates,

slaves who pledge allegiance to a strip of cloth
because obedience is a demand
and belief a sacred duty
for the slaves of the war machine.

We cheer when Jesus strides into the temple
and overturns the tables of the money changers,
freeing the speculators from their speculations
and the flashing silver from the tables of tabulation,
setting loose the spirit of God from stocks and bonds,
from the stockades and the bombs, letting loose
the holy rapture of heavenly flesh for heavenly love.

*

The archeologist brushes dust out of her long, thinning hair.
The wisdom of the ages has been inscribed on every mote—
we can hardly decipher cryptic sighs, half-rhymes,
the soft clang of a sistrum clanking.

She opens the book on the desk, finds herself wreathed in smoke.
She is in the library at Alexandria. She is burning in Egypt.
Exiles here, exiles there, refugees who never return,
the long nostalgia of the lost native land,
the poets whose perfect poems were lost to time,

so many lives a wisp gone up in remembrance
of all the was once fresh, drifted into the abyss.

The poems return in fragments on ancient papyrus
wrapped around mummies buried on the Upper Nile river,
scraps complete with worm holes in the text— o-o-o-o,
Sappho's half-sentences, her unintentionally elegiac phrases
etched on hulks found in mounds, enwrapped bones,
alpha collapsing into omega, eros into thanatos,
a constant wind from the desert tearing at the edges.

The living pass over borders
in yellow smoke, in red zones,
on their way to green zones.

The dead pass from the light,
hoping to hear an answering cry.

*

It is time that we left
to join the procession. Soon,
we will sail from Upper Egypt down into Cairo.
Then we will be lost in the maze of streets,
in the bazaar of the ordinary
accompanied by the shrill shouts of shopkeepers.
We will bargain for our fate
at the gate of the gatekeeper,
at the entrance to the unknown
in a time we can't choose, old friend,
under a red sky with a blue moon,

and the gods will look upon us
and they will smile at our tears.

II

In the rhythm and blues darkness, deep in the poverty deserts
with Johnny and the Lost Souls, listening to Radio Baghdad.

Nights of the Seven Pillars of *Boca de Loca*—
seventh son of the seventh day—
                    (Ask Septimus,
                            paranoid antenna raised,
                            why are the birds singing?

        Why are the birds singing in Arabic?

        The old songs are scribbled
        between stars, skywriting
        across desert skies.

                Aldebaran in a bull's eye
                — he's following the seven sisters
                        now there're six)

Doxologies drift unheard in distant firmaments.
Mercury's in transit and neon veins dazzle.

The messengers proselytize in sulphurous hospital light.
In a deeply wounded time, morphine drips from syringes,
pain killers snipe from a great distance.
                    "You won't feel a thing."

        Cheerleaders of war— eyes glistening with pride—
        run back and forth across the stage
        draped with massive flags
        while striped ranks clash in the dark.

        These nights of horse.
        These knights of despair.
        Nights by the Tigris, nights by the tail.
        Nights in towns, nights in beds,
        nightmares of gunships, conquests.

        They recite prayers we never hear,
        those people over there, wearing
        face scarves in the duststorm,
        clothed in robes and sandals
        like characters in the Bible.

        Listeners gather along the river
        They hear the water. They see
        what they want to see— a savior
        to tell them they may yet find hope
        in a desert here, a desert there,
        in a desert as bleak as eternity.

*

In the night, we arrive, crusaders
on a mission we cannot recollect,
following orders we forget.
There was a heap of uncertainty
about the sure thing that was going
to save us— a definite presence
of a mystical advent, about
as likely as rain in the desert.

What is that song saying? Who is singing?
Diminished sevenths— the elders and the priests
prefer the thief to the savior. The American viceroy
wears a suit, a tie, and hiking shoes,
smears of shit on the sole,
a role for a Roman named Pontius Pilate,
for an overseer of a colony
with a penchant for expediencies—
order, organization and clean hands—
the methods of oil execs from the Permian Basin
with their gushing enthusiasm
while ghostly bands, soldiers
and resisters do the Texas two-step—
"Now you're alive, now you're dead…"

There's a human name on someone lips, one of the dead,
one of the numberless dead, as if they lived, as if through
these nights a lost child listened, nights a lost son
tuned into Babylonian Radio, as if

        we could finally end

          nights like this.

*

Cities on the war map wonder if they'll get away with it.
    New York didn't. Madrid didn't. London didn't.
    In Paris, the death metal cult went for it.
    A comic operetta, they named a theatre for it— *Bataclan*.

    A pageant, I guess, blood on the seats, blood in the wings,
    blood on the stairs, blood, blood, blood.

Mediterranean stations loop through static
Electronic blips and prolonged screams.
Stockhausen reacted to The Twin Towers as if slaughter
asymmetrically invoked the Italian Futurists.
        (speed and machine gunners in the abattoir)
We'll need to re-arrive in *arriviste* gear
in order to revise the theory of the avant-garde.

Trailing bandages, trailing theories,
conflicting reports blurt from Algerian flutes, Sudanese attitudes.

    "These upstarts appear out of nowhere—
    who's in charge?"

    Folded so often, the maps begin to tear.
    The rivers are red, the rivers are running with blood.

    Nights thick with tough talk and sharp stars.
        Homeric rags hung on broken shields,
        hollers over busted swords,
        blues for the warriors, blues
        embued with voices
        full of heroic metrics
        that always count
        Agamemnon stiff,
        Agamemnon numb,

        Agamemnon sick,
        Agamemnon dumb.

The dead are lying, like it or not.
Dying of lies, swarmed by flies.

    "See," he said gleefully, pointing
    to the dead dog, grinning hideously—

    "Look at the whiteness of the teeth!"

Teachers are like that.
Prophets arrive unexpectedly.
The twists of wit are instructive.

But there's no mirth in Mississippi,
no more fun in Tennessee,
no more sandalwood burning on an altar.
Just a bunch of smoldering tires.
A jar of myrrh, a jug of red wine,
a loaf of Wonder Bread, a long rest
for the wicked who instigate war, Omar.

Why are the birds singing in Arabic?
Why are the women wailing?

Just a lot of smoking rubber and scorched soles,
scorched souls floating down the Euphrates.

Occasional spits— flitting flames around belted steel radials.
Not exactly frankincense, the oil burns in the tired engines.

It's no solace for the corpses in Atocha Station.
The ambulances come rushing.
No bell-ringing can bring back the deafening absences.
London, Madrid, Baghdad, the Twin Towers—
we are sliding down columns of smoke,
we are lost in paragraphs of the articles of war,
and the only one paying attention to the Iraqi about to be murdered
on the floor of the mosque in Fallujah is
the American with the gun walking over to finish him off.

No matter the hands waving, raised in helplessness.
No matter the fingers of those waving hopelessly from the rubble.
No matter the palms waving in surrender from the car
shot up by the contractors hired by Blackwater,
the bodies sliding down the banks of the two rivers—

> the nightmare rivers,
> the unrelenting grief
> when the telegram comes,
> when the uniformed men
> walk across the lawn,
> ghosts in the porch shadows
> and down the apartment halls
> ghosts in the wind— torn souls.
> Few will remember how the war began,
> how it came to its end,
>
> a whirlwind spinning
> back and forth
> across a barren plain.

III

The rest of the world goes on as it always has,
living with that big, crazy neighbor down the block,
the one with the black pickup in the drive
or the oversized Suburban with tinted glass,
the one who flies flags and huffs gas,
the one who hides behind blinds
and sometimes peeks and sometimes
draws a bead, follows a target
while grievance rises in proportion
to unrealized love. Seventy million homes with guns.
Someone's coming to take something from them.
Spinning a dial like a rising and falling half-mandala,
you might just catch God on Worldwide Radio.

He's waiting for you to contact him
because he wants to exonerate you for any of your sins.

> In search of oil, in search of pearls,
> In search of a diamond, in search of a spiral.

> In search of a sermon, in search of a light,
> In search of an entrance, in search of lies.
> In search of a chant, in search of a war,
> In search of losses, in search of excuses,
> In search of an exit, in search of coffins,
> In search of a solution, in search of the obvious.

Monomanical monorail of monolithic monotheism,
white star, bright star, red star, dwarf star,
star of plunder, star of blight, star of night
after night after night, westward leading,

still proceeding, guide us to a hymn of praise
and a delusion of order by closing the border.

> Ambient waves rebound from the atmosphere,
> resounding in waves of cosmic dust,
> in the milk of the Milky Way,

in myriad star particles that belittle our sun
and in the vast static that attends the Void.
It might be broadcasting even now as I write.
A few times, I have tuned-in to the aeolian spheres.
The walls will fall down when you change the sound.
Or so the prophet says. Did the prophet know?

123 in Baghdad yesterday.

126 tomorrow.

Draw a line in the sand.

After the next sandstorm arrives,
draw another line.

You don't need to stand in Jerusalem to know
which way the sand blows.
The Abrahamic folk,
the People of the Book, know.
They know all, see all, tell all
the rest of us what to do,
how to do it.
Nothin' to it.

There are two rivers running down from the far mountains
and through the cities of the plain to the sea,

two rivers of right, three rivers of wrong,
and a strongarm mentality that runs amok among us.

Let's brush up on the etiquette of the Kalashnikov.
Let's review the navigation of the dhow
as we go overland, tacking through sand
until we find ourselves in unknown circumstances.

There are no ships in the desert—
only mirages of water,
shallow promises of deliverance.

It may be the secret life in the eternal war—
a long trek on an endless road
where no road goes. The warriors
must walk the world without directions
to abandoned villages, where signs
point further to somewhere

on a mission to keep going,
barefoot and thoughtless in a land of cactus,
lip-syncing prayers
under a tyranny that can't stop
hiding behind the camouflage of God.

We must slow and locate ourselves,
look down and find our hands in the dream.

This is a land of ancient cities.
There were prominent landmarks
that once stood right over there
even if where they used to be,
before the bombing,
remains in the agitated mind
yet to find its way.

Now this block is atop that block
and a building once stood tall where this pit yawns.

*

On Babylonian Radio,
the singers are smooth,
the singers are gravel-throated,
the singers are larks,
the singers are numbed with grief.

Deserts there, deserts here,
deserts of old deserted cities,
deserts of sandstone cliffs
where the hawks nest— this song
is dedicated to everyone out there

in Ur, in Juarez, on the border,
in the nether regions of the third world,
the seven seas, the islands flooding
and the forests burning furiously,
dedicated to the *chicanas* who phone-in
to recite boyfriend names at the bomber base
and to all the subversive herd boys
beyond Lake Van in the north—
to waves so short, life so long, war so frequent
and streets that run off in the circuit suburbs
on the hills over the border in the *maquiladoras*
where third-world women crowd the lines,
sauter connections, weave the wires, assemble components
for dissembling speculators lost in the points of profits.
This song is dedicated to the other prophets
who are full of loss, the prophets
in the watchtowers, the cosmic seers
who foresee the fall and cry:
"Babylon! Babylon has fallen!"

*

This song is dedicated to those awaiting falling bombs,
to those crouched in basements and bunkers,
under the Japanese, German, Russian guns,
under the American guns.
This song is dedicated to the others, the ones
who endure the long silences of prisons,
to the Uighurs of Xinjiang and the Tibetans,
to all the "criminals" of conscience detained
by the oligarchs of communism, capitalism, corruption,
to every sufi swirling circuitous robes
who trance-dance to raise the ghosts in Syrian cities
lying in rubble,
to the refugees swarming towards the northern borders
and going under by the hundreds in the unforgiving seas,
huddled along the barbed wire of the Hungarian fascists
and in the shadows of the high walls across Texas,
New Mexico, Arizona,
refugees of the twentieth and twenty-first centuries
on this universal wheel of grind and agony that spews songs
of woe on the short wave, the long wave, the broken roads.

*

Sunset reflects in many windows across the river.
Darkness descends, lights go out across the world.

On Babylonian Radio, we sing ourselves to sleep.
On Babylonian Radio, the wind sings with dust,

and dust covers the gardens. Only rain brings rebirth.
but the rains have stopped falling— they never come down.
The people aren't listening. Even the mystics
fall into deep sleep and stop twirling.

Dust dances in cylinders, dancing dust devils,
whirling dervishes of war who hear no music.

From somewhere, someone comes floating on a log
a round of wood where they stand with a limb
and stroke their way along an imaginary river
from an imaginary forest in a vast desert.

If you stay still and pay attention
you may be able to hear a radio station
that plays the sound of rain.
It is a far-off signal often drowned by static.
They say it comes from Ur.
They say it comes from the moon.
They say you can hear water falling
in the interstices of time,
but you cannot turn centuries of neglect
into hanging gardens
or live through these long droughts and endless wars
and thirst for something beyond shallow mirages.
Deliverance wavers and blurs in the distances,
an oasis we stumble upon
only to find bedraggled palms, a dry spring.
Without the rhythm of water music,
no one dances in Babylonia anymore.

*

An arc appeared
with the slightest upward curve.

The arc was Iris in her delicate colors
and she soared off the battlefields,

out of the frames of myriad screens
and the bounded limitations of no-man's land,

a curve off the curvature of the earth
and into thin air, where clouds gather,

and the arc carried the souls and the spirits aloft,
who were lighter than air, and they rode high

across the stratosphere, free of the gravity
that had saddled them below,

until they fell, riding inside the rain, falling
through light and refracting, the *arco iris*,

the arch in the sky banded with colors.
They descended, as the rainbow descends,

a bridge to the earth, a path to the water,
a drop in the vast cycle of the river

that might lead back into something— as if
miracles happened, and we all lived again

happily ever after.

In the Water

John Reed's Lost Poem

My grandfather piped gas
to light-up red-barked cedar trees.
My grandmother loved to dance outside
all through a summer night
in a Portland, Oregon backyard.
Forest moths fell like maple leaves.

When it rained, transpacific schooners
slipped downriver past peaks. I'd imagine
the soft cries of Shanghaied sailors
bound in the hold of Astoria's deep fogs,
or the invisible tail of the last otter
slapping a glassy sea. Fins in the current,
canoe oars and the paddle wheels of fish weirs
turning in Columbia waters.

Tin pants and spiked boots in the woods-
men drove mules, mules pulled logs
along muddy skids. Tough foremen
drove lines of women in salmon canneries.

You could hear God damn
in the whang- a saw blade,
or the wail of a young woman
cut-to-the-quick by each and every man
in the all-night brothel on the wharf.
Spiked tones of Cantonese
sang-song from iron wheels
on railroads running east

to meet the foreign vowels,
the poor masses of Europeans
whose immigrant throats shouted "STRIKE!"
when rattling lines of looms ceased
in shut-down mills at Paterson and Lowell.

       Police horses clopped,
       clubs thudded
       dull on skulls.

In Our Town

Downtown at noon, a maestro taps a glass with a spoon,
a woman twirls with an umbrella emblazoned with stars,
a wit recites Roberts Rules of Order by talking in tongues,
and a cat dances with a small dog on their hind legs.

In our town, the poets write haikus

in white ink on red maple leaves
and send them floating to likely readers downriver
in Corvallis, Salem, Portland and Astoria.

Here, the graffiti artists use invisible ink
and the billboards only present original art
without any intention to sell anything
except delight, enigma, surprise, and shock.

There are a large number of musicians around,
and they play light refractions that arc in a spectrum,
colors that are meleodic lines, songs that illuminate
the black and white enigmas of everyday life.

If you need a guide, we have trained and licensed
scat singers who enjoy leading you around
to see if they can confound your tendency
to want everything exact and clearly communicated.

In the late evening, you will meet hallucinogenic refugees
who have arrived by astral projection in the midst of the mall,
and they carry passports that enable them to slip through
the walls and the vaults, the jails and the crypts.

It is no small trick that we were born to swim,
so we have creeks instead of streets, pools
where there used to be crossroads, and outer wear
that is like a tattoo but runs in the rain— watery sleeves.

A nice place to live, a better place to drift.

*

As a teen, Richard Brautigan used to fish the ponds right off Highway 99 in north Eugene. He'd stand on a shoulder, sway in the wake of semis whapping past, cast out his line and ponder the lack of a plop when the sinker splashed. He couldn't hear subtleties above the roar of traffic, so what might have been the essence of the most famous of Basho's haikus— the sound of a frog diving into a pond—was drowned by honking horns, gunned engines, downshifting trucks, and loudmouths screaming at the kid on the side of the road as they drove pickups to Junction City.

After high school, trying to be a writer in Eugene in the 1950s, Brautigan pushed the limits and went hungry. There wasn't much sympathy. As his daughter Iolanthe relates in a biography of her father, he lost weight, grew weary, and, finally, turned himself in at the police station, asking to be arrested. They laughed at him and said he'd have to commit a crime to be in jail and eat. So, he walked outside, picked up some stones, and started throwing them through the windows of City Hall. The police arrested him. A judge determined Brautigan was crazy and sent him to the state mental hospital in Salem, where he spent some months undergoing electro-shock treatments for his desire to write, his need to survive. When he was released, he immediately hitch-hiked south on 99 to San Francisco. He never returned to Oregon.

*

If and when— subjunctive strands
of philosophical speculation cast into the river,
fine lures spun in the face of a pulling current,
lifelines of nearly invisible thread
that remain impractical.
Yet they catch real cutthroat on fake flies,
wherein lies a comma that splices entire sentences
together— lives
that depend on what if and maybe when,
a possibility that doesn't exist, but does
when minute life swims into moon light,
another whopper of a fish story that can't be believed
from here to Mississippi, yet a circumstance
that yields real people in a real world.

The Golden Road Ahead

We wander past the cages,
we wander through refrains,
we wander past the mechanisms
that attach windshield wipers to rain

or wider, softer tires to sand,
or dreams where a strange seacoast,
conifers above tropical plants,
draws you into unconscious waters.

A right eye peers to find the future
and it's always future perfect
because we're forever rich,
blessed with spaciousness
even if we lack requisite vision,
and addled loose change
clanks in xenophobic brains.

Goodbye, Uncle, so long, Hired Hands.
Ta, ta, faithful dog, fare thee well, Aunt Em.

You pile the brush, topple the logs,
spark with a live wire, and—*voila!*—
we're all lit up like a protesting monk.

The Tin Man laughs with a creak.
The Lion roars with a screech.
The scarecrow rocks on his sticks
(though Raven was never taken in).

Goodbye to the cedar, so long to the fir,
adieu to the ice that rings our caps.
and to a lot more than that!

Step right up, don't be timid,
we're relieved of our limits.

This will prove illuminating,
and we'll surely be centered,
well-versed, well-intentioned,
though a bit prone to wilting
when we start melting.

Lookout

You once could read enigmatic mysteries
about floods in the Pacific Northwest,
milky water from the glaciers
running dirty brown through the valleys-
the whole journey from the nipple to the sea.

Now, by August, in the heat and the lightning,
stream beds trickle past dry rock and dead moss.
Smoke from wild fires obscures everything.
Backpacking through the mountains,
something is burning, and you can't breathe.

The old fire Lookouts are gone.
The azimuth is a device for divination.
Conflagrations burn through summer into autumn,
all the way until the first rain comes, later every year.
The future isn't pretty.
The past has been pretty awful itself.

Far to the south and east,
the shills rewrite environmental laws
in black oil on ghostly drive-in movie screens,
horror flicks twisted by Texas logic
that fractures the rock below
into earthquakes, profits,
sulphur-fume faucets.
Posada skeletons sit
in their cars, attached to speakers,
dressed in their Sunday best
to recite the scriptures
while tumbleweeds pile-up on fences
and a brazen head blares out blessings.

After I come down from the mountains,
I'll go to Chinatown, hide in an alley
and watch America fall
at the end of the Ming,
the end of the Q'ing,
the end of the bling dynasty.

Extinctions

In my other life, I am a resourceful piano tuner
who can adjust the chromatics of rainbows
to tiers of sound and suture holes in the ozone.

In my other life, I am a young girl
in a big city who likes to bike through traffic
and run red lights.

In my other life, I am a pickpocket
who lifts an identity that isn't his
smooth as wind with dark intent.

In my other life, I am a contortionist
who is able to escape from a vision of the future
without grasping the meaning.

In my other life, I am a platonic radio station
that only plays perfect compositions.
Don't listen- you'll affect it.

In my only life, I am an iceberg
drifting further and further alone.
But I am hopeful.

Inferno in the American Forest

A telephone rings in the middle of the night.

"Get out now!" a friend yells.

They leave in slippers and robes, a down jacket,
a hooded rain poncho covered in ashes, a silly hat.

They drive the canyon road through fire—
sparks billowing across the windshield.

*

Last millennium's vehicle frame rusts,
bare ribs in a desert of remaining hulks,
a desert of refrains: cars, wars, massive burnings.
These are depictions, re-creations, *simulacra*
or the lasting evidence stored in every head.
Sometimes, memory, turning and turning
in its widening labyrinth, will recall
the momentary thrall, or the dismay,
the broken remnant of what was to be different.

Here is a hole where an eye could be seen,
there a siren— warning, blaring.
A gush of conjured smoke, a distorting mirror,
peroxided pulley and winch
manipulated to accentuate
the beast within, as a circus might celebrate
the roar of the big cats, the howl of clowns,
the enormous gasp when Christ the Acrobat leaps
into the ring, and the lions feast.

*

In time, flesh turns to marble.
In time, we are ground into particles.
In time, you never quite get around to considering the tight spaces

where we must contain ourselves, compounded
limitations, boundaries, borders, bigotry and tall walls
to pretend security, to restrict.

There is no salvation,
no rescue, no exit.
The heat's rising, the trees dying,
the earth cracks under the sun's blaze.
Your throat turns dry and sore
from all the smoke
as your mind splits, aches
in the face of tomorrow

on a voyage to hell, cast adrift
in a sea of fire, a sea of ennui,
helplessly lost in a time
of fear and death,
division and hate,
going under waves of disease,
the voices crying,
"I can't breathe."

Thirsty for Ancient Verities

The teacher came to the desert until the desert dawned on the teacher.
He got lost in an expanse he couldn't refute or deflect.
Infinity pities nobody, and everyone hates to admit it.
Once we understand, we fall through chaos into emptiness.

Caverns echo. Water speaks of dreams.
Novels consist of chapters I can't begin to read.

Gambling's a game. Life's a gamble every day.
If you decide to pirate the old growth cedars,
you'll live in the wasteland your heroism brings.
Your temple will soar, but no birds sing.

The born-again man renews his faith in a fixed system
by praying, by babbling about success and the reason
we go to war to set everything right, a wrong
that will be overcome, or some other long story. Christ.

They lurch into deserts without a sense of direction.
They lose themselves in sandstorms and uniforms.
Thirsty for ancient verities, the fall will be cool but dry
after the mountains burn and the seas vaporize.

Not to be lost wanderers on journeys far from home,
There may still be time left when we sit on a ledge
high above a thread, a canyon river, and hear distant whispers,
Pines above, rapids below, clouds sailing over distant plateaus.

Turn over a page, turn over a leaf, get out of the chair,
walk downstairs,
Back out into the street, open the glove box in the syllable,
Take out love, look in the rear view mirror and remember:
I'm always beside you, riding with you: a revolving dolphin
shape-shifting the concrete boulevards into flowing streams,
a crusty old geezer swimming against destructive ennui.

Dancing through Apertures

Fourth to sixth grade:
push the furniture aside,
turn out the lights,
put on the percussion, start
floating and jumping.

My father did not like
the way I danced.

If you relax and move,
stay faithful to rhythm's register,
allow yourself latitude, not a little attitude,
you must still surrender to succeed as a dancer.

Sideways spinning may draw rings around the room
and swirl into whirls— breathtaking grooves.

When you dance well for a long time,
there's nothing like it. After a spell,
you catch your second-wind,
then ride the rhythm all the way to the end.

When you get there, tell them I sent you.

*

"You need finger-cymbal rings that really ring," a belly dancer said, "and the best ones are made by a guy in Cambria, California. He takes apart old, landline phones— there's a special bell inside he uses to forge the finger-cymbal."

Anyway, I called him, and he said, 'I'll be glad to do it, if you'll do something for me.'"

"What?"

"I've got cancer, I'm dying, and I need some shrooms. Can you get me some?"

"Oh, I'm so sorry... Sure, I'll be glad to. How many?"

"As much as you can," he said.

So, the next day, I went out to a cow pasture I know in the Skagit Valley and found a ring of mushrooms. I started picking with

167

my fingers and filling a flat cap I had worn there. After a while, I guess the substance was absorbed through my fingertips. I realized I was getting high! It was such a beautiful day— fleeting white clouds chased by the sun with the wind sweeping waves across the spring grasses. I was laughing at myself, but also thinking of the ring-maker.

"Later, I found myself crying, standing in the wind, looking east to the North Cascades covered in snow. The peaks were bannering spindrift like ocean waves in an offshore wind. But it was an onshore wind, a west wind, and I thought of Shelley's poem, and I thought of my dying friend, and the wonder life is, until it isn't. But it's also forever, just like that, just like this."

         *

High-flying flocks,
snow cloud wisps,
blue peaks—
waves move
mountains in the sea.

In dawn's long,
slant-shadowing sun,
the discerning eye
catches a glimpse—
spiralling spindrift's
quick iridescence
off breaking waves—
a rainbow spray.

What are you reading
when you read the sea?

I see distant storms,
and I ride waves
from storms
thousands of
miles away.
Tell me, what are
you dreaming
when you dream
The Book of the Sea?

I dream I am reading
the scroll of the waves,
the visionary waves
that rise in eternity
to break in eternity,
one great volume
on the beach.

Dolphin Found Dead

Taking to swimming by following my mother,
I learned to surf inside the waves
but forgot to limit my leaping
from the ocean. In my exuberance,

I came down from one great high,
impaled myself on a white picket fence.
Christ of the Waters, I was crucified
in a garden on a hill above the sea.

Out in the Water

Out in the water, you learn patience,
wait for a set, try to be in the right place
to slide into it. Out in the water,
there's likeable silence
to a gliding line of pelicans
riding invisible updrafts
on unbroken waves.
Out in the water, you heed
the sound of surf: the hiss
of spindrift, the crack of a lip
and the roaring break— this
happens fast— and the hiss
again, when foam on the water
sizzles as it disappears.
You have to be near,
close to listen to what it says
in another language altogether.
Out in the water, it can be baffling—
the casual look you give
to a nearby, surfacing seal.
You don't understand— you can't
look them in the eye. They get riled,
and sometimes they'll charge you,
try to knock you off your board.
It's simply who they are,
out in the water.
A looming swell rises,
uncoils in a spiral
like the storm that spawned it,
born of wind—
like-to-kind, akin.
Catching a mountain
moving in the sea,
you finesse turns,
tilts, timing
to keep riding,
guiding the board
in a dance

with the wave
and its power
out in the water.

Night Work

Beyond the tent fly
a shaker of stars spill on sand-

dew drops in the flashlight beam.
An old man like me
must get up in the night to

walk out on the deserted beach:
          low tide
    while the moon rides high
    in sunless sky.

        Starfish shine
    in the book of night-
        a boulder gleams.

Voices in the surf break
future-past and future-perfect,

    voice of a tern,
    voice in a dream,
    cri, cri, cri.

There are no words
when you fall back asleep
to the sound of waves,
        only thin pages
        printed with ripples
        over a transparency,

  currents that leave riddles

             flakes.

Columbia River Elegy

While philosophers squabble over spirit and flow,
A stone cutter carves a wavy line for water,
Two more to mirror the river.
Empty boat in a Tlakluit song,
A fish net with a long tear that needs mending.

I'll weave you a straw hat
for your last journey down the Gorge
all the way from your home in The Dalles
to the raging Pacific at the mouth,
and you won't require a pilot
to cross those treacherous bars.

Being a master of navigating *dharma*,
you will find your way through
cross-currents, spinning eddies, ocean tides,
and long swells that roll thousands of miles
with a silent hidden energy.

Despite the chaos and anarchy in all ten directions,
not to mention the roar, the winds,
the spume left floating from the spindrift,
and the water-logged logs
that tore the keels off wooden ships,

It's tranquil in a room at Laguna Honda
where you float like you were sailing
over the waves, over the container ships
full of emptiness and echoes of emptiness.

A far-off temple bell resounds
in the ear of a migrating crane,
a great whale dives deep
in the blameless sea.

Zen Attitude

In the face of cataclysmic change
when the end of the world is reckoned
and a medical chart with your name points
somewhere off the virtual page, you
can still take solace in the wide world
where the Rhone runs a course from the Alps,
the Ganges from Tibetan snows,
and an Indian sage with one earring
forever sails the Yangtze, standing on a reed.

As if you could still plot an escape
to the Oregon cloud breaks you once surfed
beyond fir and cedar capes, blue walls
to sweep, riding high but staying deep
to climb and dive and climb, a curl
over a shoulder, a roar in the wake.

Attached to the radiation platform
on a steel bed, there is a helmet of stiff mesh
screwed to fix your targeted head.
Chemo on Fridays, Saturdays in a ditch.
The brain is to blame for almost everything.

I've lost a lot of weight, not to say strength.
The Oregon beach breaks? I won't navigate
going round and round over indefinite reefs
with shifting sand's uncharted contingencies.
Existence is canceling me.

I remember when, over a loudspeaker
on a crowded holiday train, no food,
the French conductor said, with a laugh:
"Adopt a Zen attitude."

Harbinger

After five days below freezing,
in a crisp realm of ice, clear skies
and distant southern light,
the only fly seen in weeks appears fake
as it stands on the kitchen floor
in a shaft of weak sunshine.

I lean down and salute the little pest—
the hungry fly that can no longer fly,
tiny survivor, improbable teacher,
ancient of his days, last of his time.

Dusk

White rose petal,
early September,

a white spider
on white velvet—

pure as winter's
long night to come.

*

In old age, at night,
you feel light,

light enough to lift
from the bed

and drift
through fields beyond.

*

The nice part about dying—
you don't have to think
too far ahead.

Vow

I'd ride the rise and fall of the world,
breathing in to finally breathe out,
and lay myself to rest
with an old hymn going around in my head,

a hymn that has nothing to do
with jealous gods or Christian soldiers,
or some glorious ascension to
heavenly streets paved with gold.

It will have to be something
from a natural testament:
a western meadowlark
singing to a morning field,
a grove of red cedars
hiding an invisible stream,
a spoken poem, a soft breeze.

\

For Chris

We eat peaches packed-in from the valley,
go for a walk along the water,
hurl dark pits as far as we can. I grab a stray log
thinking ahead to tonight's fire— how did it ever
get all the way up here? Standing at a col, you ask:
"How long it has been since we looked out over Nevada?"
I'm falling in love with her all over again, the woman
I brought here forty years ago. It must be the light
she carries into the wilderness, high on a ridge
beside a cairn. She says she fell in love with me
because I took her to snow in August, made her
a Kool-aid snow cone. In the afternoon, sitting
below a pass, next to the same snowfield
shrinking at the end of summer, the end
of the Anthropocene, I pour a dry stream
of garishly colored powder onto a scooped peak
in a tin cup. Sharing it back and forth,
it's more than big enough for the two of us.

Under the Dome

Under the dome, circling Polaris,
we travel together through a lifetime,
climbing steep trails to find lookouts,
floating down one river after another,
driving the streets, drowning in traffic,
awakening to dreams clear as a bell.

We come inside, out of the cold,
when October winds clarify constellations,
grateful for walls and feathered quilts,
a longtime couple, growing old, slowly adrift,
forgetful cartographers of the infinite.

Poet, translator of poetry from Spanish, essayist, Paul Dresman was born in southern California in 1943. A conscientious objector during the Vietnam War and an activist for a range of causes, he co-edited *Crawl Out Your Window* (with Rex Pickett and Mel Freilicher) and bilingual *helicóptero* (with Chilean poet Jesús Sepúlveda).

Dresman taught literature and writing at the University of California at San Diego, at Beijing Teachers' University in China (invited by poet Zheng Min), and at the University of Oregon— where he lives in Eugene.

In 2020, he won the poetry award of the San Miguel Writers' Conference.

11/09 ★ 09/11

EL SUR ES
AMERICA

1973 ★ 2023

Made in United States
Troutdale, OR
08/22/2023

12296928R10104